Endorsements

Walter Jordan has not lived in his hometown of Fort Wayne, Indiana for some time now; but the very mention of his name still evokes a smile to the eyes of those who know him. He does that to people. As a former local sportswriter, I knew Walt when he was a gangly forward on his high school basketball team, he led to the state championship in 1974. He was all arms, elbows, and knees back then - a kid with a flash of brilliance who went onto an all-Big Ten career at Purdue, and then the NBA, although injuries ended his tenure prematurely. In his book you will find it is not in Walt's nature to accept defeat or despair. You will read about his tireless work, compassion, zest, passion, faith and love for young people, his family, and community! Read his story. Hear what is within his heart, I am quite sure that your eyes will also smile at the mention of his name!

—**Steve Warden**
Sports Editor
Journal Gazette

Through the years, Walter Jordan has been a tremendous source of encouragement to me personally. In writing this book Walt continues to speak hope, reassurance, and inspiration into my life. Walt and I grew up together in the inner-city of Fort Wayne, IN. We became best friends at the tender age of five years. When Walt told me, he was writing a book about his life's journey I was thrilled. I was thrilled because Walter indeed has a powerful story to tell. Walt's success as an athlete, entrepreneur, and human being did not happen overnight. It was a journey that required sacrifice, commitment, perseverance, motivation, inner fortitude, strength of character, and faith. This book invites you into the journey. A journey that I am certain will leave you, as it did me, inspired.

—**Pastor Raymond Causey**
Urban Family Ministry
Pastor Redemption

Coach Jordan has always been like a second father to me. He is truly an amazing display of character and what a Godly man is. Coach Jordan has taught me so many life lessons that I still carry with me today. I am excited for others to get a glimpse into the amazing life this man has led by impacting others.

—**Hunter Henry**
University of Arkansas Grad
College All-American
New England Patriots, TE

Coach has been a second father since the day I met him. Growing up basketball was always second, Coach Jordan's main concern was developing character which makes sense because his is second to none. His impact on those around him is undeniable and I am so thankful that he is sharing his journey to impact even more people than he already has.

—**Dustin Ware**
University of Georgia Grad
Professional Basketball Player

Walter Jordan there are no words that can adequately describe how blessed I am to have this man in my life and being one of my biggest role models and supporters my entire life. He is always seeking to inspire and uplift others.

Always see the potential and the best in others. A man who speaks truth to power, no matter who like it or not. I am so proud of you big fella! I love you more than any words I can ever say. May God continue to bless your journey as you continue to inspire and motivated others to get the best out of their journeys. Your life too will be enrich by his journey! Get the book!

—Joe Jordan
National Executive of The Year (2 years)
Executive Director Boys & Girls Club
College Hall of Fame - All American

I have known Walter Jordan for my entire life. He has an uncanny ability to identify tough issues, lead, pull together individuals to help address challenges and impact others. He has always made himself accessible to others in need; and willing to help when and where he could. Walter Jordan is a compelling storyteller with the gift of animating his life experiences, to encourage, motivate and inspire young and old!

—Fred Arrington
Purdue University Grad
Former NFL Player
CEO – Corporate Executive

- Wilma -

Thanks for your
Service!! Make true good

Lord richly BLESS YOU!!

. BLESSINGS!

#34

GOD BLESS!

GRACEFULLY
BROKEN

PASSION **DROVE** HIM
COMPASSION **GUIDED** HIM

WALTER JORDAN

A HALL OF FAMER'S TRUE STORY

FREILING
PUBLISHING

Published by Freiling Publishing,
a division of Freiling Agency, LLC.

P.O. Box 1264,
Warrenton, VA 20188

www.FreilingPublishing.com

ISBN 978-1-950948-84-0

Printed in the United States of America

Table of Contents

Foreword

I AM HONORED TO WRITE THIS short testimonial about the author, Walter Jordan. I do believe that, more than anyone else, I am qualified to give you a glimpse of the man, the journey and the Hall of Famer. I've known him all of his life. He is my younger brother, the seventh of ten children. When he told me he was writing this book, I couldn't have been more pleased because he has a compelling story that needs to be told.

As you read this book you'll see that Walter's life journey was just that . . . a journey. One that had its ups and downs, twists and turns, celebrations and disappointments. I've watched him as he would press his way through each challenge and still remain on the journey. I've always been amazed at his resilience, and his ability to absorb the blows of life while maintaining a positive outlook. I realized that, somewhere along the way, he learned to enjoy the journey as well as the destination.

When I attended Walt's induction into the Indiana Basketball Hall of Fame, I remember telling a family friend, Oakley Causey: "*They are just recognizing him as a Hall of Famer **today**, but Walt has been a Hall-of-Famer in life since he was a teenager back on Masterson Street*". Oakley simply nodded in agreement. All of his life, on and off the court, Walt never crowded the front for well deserved recognition and praise. He didn't go through life asking, *"What's in it for me?"* Instead he constantly asked, *"What can I do to help?"*

When I look back over my brother's journey, I'm reminded of a quote from the great Maya Angelo: *"You may encounter many defeats, but you must not be defeated. In fact, it may be necessary to encounter the defeats, so you can know who you are, what you can rise from, how you can still come out of it."*

Walt will tell you that he's been guided by his faith and his family. This divine combination worked together to shape his world view. His family and his faith taught him the value of PASSION and COMPASSION. Over the years, this drove him to use his journey experiences to directly help thousands of young people develop a sense of pride and dignity. Passion drove him, but compassion guided him. He is a hero to the countless number of young people he coached, mentored, advised and encouraged.

This book, Gracefully Broken, is appropriately titled. As you read, you'll see how he is able to thank God for both, the broken times and the times of victory. As you read, you will appreciate how Walt is able to use the broken times to improve and increase his level of service to elevate the human condition.

—Charles Jordan

CHAPTER 1

How in the Hell Did I Get Here?!

IT WAS A VERY COLD DAY on January 25, 1975. It had literally been ten months from the date that I was at Indiana University's Assembly Hall (Bloomington, Indiana), leading my high school's Northrop Bruins team to the prestigious Indiana High School State Championship. The game, broadcasted to thousands all over the state, was being played in front of a sold-out crowd of seventeen thousand passionate fans, with hundreds of college coaches in attendance. Now, ten months later, this still eighteen-year-old skinny kid, who was not supposed to make it, found himself on college basketball's biggest stage, playing in one of college basketball's biggest rivalries—Purdue vs. Indiana. We were playing in front of a national television audience against the number one college team in America. That number one ranked team featured six seasoned junior players, four All-Americans (Scott May, Quinn Bucker, Bobby Wilkerson, Kent Benson), a total of six future NBA draft selections, and one of the game's best coaches ever, legendary and Hall of Fame Coach Bobby Knight.

The previous night I did not sleep very well as I kept asking myself, "How in the hell did I get here?!" As I went on with my life, little did I know that that same million-dollar question would always follow me. On deck this year were a number of future NBA players named Terry Furlow, Greg Kelser, Mychal Thompson, Phil Hubbard, Bruce King, Billy McKinney, Mark Olberding, Mark Landsberger, Flip Saunders, and Lindsay Hairston. This was along with a Big Ten powerhouse schedule (Indiana, Michigan, Michigan State, Iowa, Wisconsin, Northwestern, Illinois, Ohio State, Minnesota), as well as tough non-conference battles against such teams as California, West Kentucky, Florida State, San Diego State, Indiana State, Ball State, and West Virginia.

No matter who we were (person, team, organization, or team), we all had to overcome some degree of fear, unforeseen challenges, roadblocks, adversity, negativity, and our minds. This was pivotal in helping each of us to create a sense of resilience and a strong desire to win. It was also necessary to forge in us a desire to live out God's plan and purpose for our lives.

Being extremely poor and growing up in the heart of the inner city with nine siblings, I quickly learned that there would be plenty of times when we would get knocked down. But all that mattered was how many times could we got back up. The cold hard fact is that the only ones who have no challenges are called dead people. I would later find out that I did not know the half of it. Many challenges were straight ahead: mourning the death of my amazing mom when I was seventeen, becoming a proud father at twenty, waking up in the middle of the night and finding out that I could not walk at twenty-two, losing my only son, grieving my father's death, breaking my foot twice while in the

NBA, and having quadruple bypass heart surgery. These are just a few, but there were even more challenges to come.

As I went on to lead my Boilermaker team in scoring three out of four years, I also became a three-time All-Big Ten Performer, a two-time MVP, and a two-time captain at Purdue University. I was selected to represent the USA on the 1977 World University Games Gold Medal team, and then I played in the NBA and in Europe. I went on to become a corporate success, a community activist, a successful coach, an author, and a motivational speaker. I still found myself once again asking that million-dollar question: "How in the hell did I get here?!"

The good thing is that at the age of thirteen, I found out that I loved being a part of a team. At age seventeen, I learned that I could accomplish most of my goals. With the right teammates, circle, and mentors, I felt that I had a chance. Knowing that it would not be easy, I began to read about successful people who I admired and who had achieved at high levels against all odds. Many of this interesting cast of characters provided optimism, enthusiasm, inspiration, purpose, insights, vision, and confidence. They confirmed many of the things I had already heard repeatedly from my amazing team of childhood mentors, coaches, and family members. Many of them you will have the privilege to meet during this journey. I hope and pray they bless you as much as they have me.

In my latter years, publishers, authors, friends, business partners, former teammates, and folk who knew small parts of my journey would consistently ask me about writing a book and sharing my story. So, after a lot of prayers and procrastination, I was reminded that a blessing was only a blessing if it was passed on to someone else, like the hundreds of personal stories, authors, and books that helped me grow and gave me the inspiration, confirmation, and the extra juice I needed to keep going. I only hope and pray that this book will encourage at least one person to walk in faith instead of fear. Your blessings are not just for you!

CHAPTER 2

312 East Masterson Street

IN MY EARLY TEENAGE YEARS, I would always wonder why my family moved from house to house (six times), with each house being within a block or two of each other. One of our six landlords once told my mom that he could not rent to us because we had too many boys. Apparently, he was fearful of the damage that seven boys could do (and did) to some walls.

Because everybody in my world looked and lived as we did, it never dawned on us that we were poor. We only knew that we were taught to respect other folk, to excel in school, and to say our prayers at night. We were constantly reminded that we were special. I always felt that I was loved, even when I was being punished for my misdeeds. As such, we had everything we needed. We were not allowed to make excuses of any kind.

My strongest and fondest memories took place in our three-bedroom home at 312 E. Masterson Street. Seven boys (Willie, Charles, Lafayette, Douglas, Art, Joe, and I) all slept in one bedroom; three girls (Suzette, Diana, and Laurietta) slept in the second; and my parents slept in the other. Our days and nights were always filled with adventures and challenges. The tight quarters and physical closeness made for some interesting nightly conversations, arguments, fights, and laughs. Little did we know that we were forming unbreakable bonds that would last a lifetime.

I remember we were living at 1911 Lafayette Street when President John F. Kennedy was assassinated on November 22, 1963. When Dr. Martin Luther King and Robert Kennedy were assassinated in 1968, we were living at 312 E. Masterson. The M.L. King assassination was especially tough because my mom was a school classmate of Coretta Scott (King) as children while growing up in Alabama. I remember the tears, pain, hurt, and anger felt in our family and our entire community. As a young boy, I could not understand how some people could have so much hate in their hearts.

Looking back on those early days of my life, I am exceedingly grateful for my parents because, against all odds, they put my nine siblings and me in an environment that gave us the best chance to excel. They didn't have much money, but they made sure that the institutions in our lives were fit for the expectations, morals, and values they had set for us. The schools, the neighborhoods, and the churches all worked together to made us feel loved and protected. As I reflect, I now realize that was our wealth.

I get goose bumps thinking about those magical porches where, after dinner and a hard day's work, our parents and neighbors would walk over to each other's home to chat. After a long hard day's work, they would sit on each other's porch and exchange stories about kids, church, and work. None of us had much, but each home was always open for all of us kids. They all knew each other's kids' names and what our parents expected of us. In fact, the parents in the neighborhood had permission to discipline each other's kids when needed. The bond still lives inside of all of us, now for well over a half of century.

The families included the Hamiltons, Causeys, Wallaces, Chaneys, Kings, Arringtons, Wallaces, Sanders, Hayneses, Freemans, Martins, Flowers, Bryants, Hales, Banks, Williamses, Hicks, Nelsons, Stephenses, Chaneys, Wades, Thomases, Folks (cousins), Jordans (grandparents), and others. Every day we would witness the men coming to and from work with hard hats and lunch buckets in hand. The men left home with clean uniforms and arrived back home dirty, exhausted, and hungry. Yet they still found time to show all of us some love. Sunday was a special day, as most of our moms would get up early to start our Sunday dinners (the best and biggest meal of the week) before we all headed to Sunday school and church services. After dinner, it was time to watch the Chicago Bears or the NBA game of the week, and then we'd play hoops and hoops and hoops! Sunday was always the best day of the week.

We were blessed to see folk that looked like us running and managing their own businesses: gas stations, barbershops, grocery stores, liquor stores, bakeries, five-and-dime stores, and candy stores. Our church home (St. John Missionary Baptist) was eight blocks from our front door. Hanna Elementary School was only two blocks away. Fairfield Middle School was about two miles away, but it seemed to be ten miles away, as it was a long walk from Masterson Street! But my dream high school (Central) was only four blocks away. I will never forget that our two favorite hoop courts, the Reservoir Park and the fire station, were in the neighborhood, only a few blocks away. Playing basketball at Reservoir Park and the fire station felt as if we were in Madison Square Garden.

A huge part of our growing up was the struggle, though at the time we had no idea that the struggle was elevating us. Now that we look back, it appeared as if the whole crusade was designed to take us to a higher level, which would not have been possible without those struggles.

We never viewed them as struggles because we simply flowed from one day to the next. It became clear that what enabled us to endure was the fact that we had each other. Those seeds of greatness planted in each of us may not have manifested themselves to us in those moments, but as we got older, we understood how each of them helped us to find a way to apply them, which gave us the confidence and the ability to be strong, feel loved, have faith, and win.

CHAPTER 3

The Layup Line

HALF A CENTURY LATER, I STILL remember the day as if it were yesterday. It was a cold, zero-degree October day in Fort Wayne, Indiana. My best friend, Raymond (Ray) Causey, had just heard that our Hanna Elementary School was having basketball tryouts for our fifth-grade team. He was excited about it, and with his usual ability, he talked me into trying out with him.

Now mind you, playing basketball was not something we did in our spare time together. But on a whim, he had this brilliant idea, and I was all in. Having no clue about what to expect, I watched intently and tried to follow what the kids in front of me were doing. But it just didn't work. The coach yelled LAYUPS, and our tryouts had begun.

On my second attempt, I ran with the ball (no dribble). Suddenly, I heard the coach yell, "JORDAN!" I think you know the rest. As I got my book bag and coat, I got to thinking that Raymond was not any good either, so I decided to wait outside in the freezing cold so we could walk home together. About fifteen minutes later, my best friend came walking out. Some friend, huh?

Ray's brother, Oakley, and my three older brothers all had a passion for basketball. As we walked home, I didn't seem to get emotional until I saw how upset Ray was about getting cut. The closer I got near home, I found myself tearing up. With three older brothers and my pops, I should have known that I dared not go in the house crying. Oh, well!

Being the seventh of ten of the Jordan clan, and the middle boy (three older brothers), I had to learn quickly that I could not be thin-skinned, and it did not matter one bit that I was only twelve years old. As I entered the house with watery eyes, it did not take long. "What are you crying about, boy? What's wrong with you?"

I responded, "I got cut from the basketball team."

"WHAT! What the hell were you thinking about trying out for the basketball team? How did you expect to make the team when you never play? Were you following Ray again? If he jumped off the bridge, would you jump, too? Stop following other people, stupid! Nobody's going to give you nothing, boy! Stop crying, you sissy!"

What I thought was cruelty at twelve years old, I would later find out that those scoldings, tough love, and golden nuggets would affect and remain fresh in my mind my entire life. No free lunches and no entitlements; simply hard work. I learned to stop following folk. I learned to be tough.

I recall that over the next several days, I was teased at school for not making the team. For some strange reason, this inspired Ray and me to want to make the team and prove everybody wrong. We were then motivated to run to the neighborhood courts every chance we could. To be able to get to the courts as often and as quickly as possible, we would help each other with our daily house chores. For the next five years, we were attached at the hip. Mornings, afternoons, nights, rain, shine, or snow, we could be found at the fire station (the best outdoor court ever—with lights), neighborhood alleys, Reservoir Park, Weisser Park—wherever there was a hoop. Armed with more confidence than ever, I tried out the following year, but to no avail; I was cut again. All I wanted was to know what it felt like to wear that uniform.

Around this time, my lifetime building buddy Ray and I had fallen deeply in love with this game, even though it was not giving us any love back. I knew that if we had any hopes of making our middle school team the following year, we had to have a better game plan and bust our butts. At this point, my brilliant and gifted brother Charles, who was an awesome basketball player and a walk-on player at Indiana University, saw my newfound passion. He decided to take me under his wing and pour into me, and soon he would become my personal life coach, trainer, and mentor. It was around this time that everything that my parents and siblings had tried to instill in me finally began to sink in.

As an Indiana University and Michigan business school grad, former American Express marketing executive, a big-time executive for several corporations, a high school national speech champion several times, and current CEO and entrepreneur, Charles knows what it takes to win big. Though he was extremely tough and hard on me, I was all in. He was always one hundred percent honest with me and would tell me things I needed to hear, even when I didn't want to hear them. He had become my rock, as he always seemed to know how and what to do and say to motivate me. He has always been that way for our entire family. Whenever I have needed him, he has always been there and has never let me down.

For the rest of my life, I would constantly be reminded about what I say and what the Word of God says that I am.

CHAPTER 4

The Comedy Squad

RAY AND I WERE EXCITED (BUT fearful) as we got ready to move on to seventh grade at Fairfield Middle School. Unknown to us, we were shocked to find out that the coach was not cutting anyone, so we had twenty-two players on our team. While my best friend Raymond had improved enough to be a starter, I finally got my uniform. I played on the Comedy Squad, where the five worst players on each team got to play at halftime while the rest were in the locker rooms and the fans were out getting their hot dogs and cokes.

The peer teasing continued, but thanks to my parents, siblings, and Ray, my thinking and mindset were at a different place. I had learned the huge lesson of listening to the right people. They would encourage me to work harder and to believe in myself. They would ask me repeatedly: How bad do you want this? What is it you say you want?

Over the next two years of my middle school career, we would be blessed with two incredible black coaches who had a profound effect on our lives, on and off the court: Coach Jim Gurnell (RIP) and Coach AC Aldridge.

Both were successful and taught us so much about leadership, pride, discipline, mental toughness, teamwork, and winning.

At Fairfield, our basketball coaches made all of us play all three sports: football, basketball, and track. It was tough as we all loved football and hated track, but we were so close as a family that we made the best of it. In fact, we had only 13 or 14 players on our football roster my freshman year, and our number one goal was to not to get hurt before the basketball season started. The only game we won that year was against one of our rivals (6–0), who was undefeated and had talked trash to us all summer.

The truth is that we had several great athletes and football players on that team, so we should have been pretty good. One of those players, Fred Arrington, who grew up in the neighborhood, would later go on to play football at Purdue and the NFL. He become the only classmate and friend in which our journey took us through middle school, junior high, high school, and college together. In fact, while at Purdue the same year (1977), and I was honored to win the MVP on the basketball team, Fred became the first defensive player in Purdue history to be named MVP. In one of our favorite football stories, we were playing in front of a packed house against another one of our archrivals, Weisser Park. They had the top three sprinters in the city in their backfield, and our all-everything player Fred was playing tackle on my side of the line. As a 130-pound (dripping wet) defensive end, my job was to turn them in so Fred could make the tackles. Needless to say, that game plan didn't work too well. Fred would yell at me, "Just turn 'em in, Walt!" It was a lot easier said than done. Humph!

On the very last play of the game and the end of my football playing days, my best friend Raymond (quarterback) threw me a pass that I was able to somehow catch in the end zone for a touchdown. Even though we had just gotten beat by 30 points, I celebrated as if we had just won the game. We still tell those stories to this day.

I was just beginning to find myself when I first checked into my citizenship class and met my teacher, Ms. Betty Stein. I had no idea that she would be a huge inspiration and would make an enormous impact on my life. Directly across the street from Fairfield Middle School was the Allen County Society for Crippled Children and Adults. Every now and then, Ms. Stein would take our class there to work with those special needs children and adults. Little did I know that a beautiful little girl, Kimberly, would steal my heart. It got to the point that every Wednesday, Ms. Stein would allow me fifteen minutes to run across the street to see her. When I did not show up, she would cry, and the employees there would let me know about it. When I did get there, her smile and hugs would almost bring me to tears. As I moved on with my life ambitions, I vowed to never forget Kim.

As the basketball season approached, we were told that each player would be wearing and had to purchase Chuck Taylor tennis shoes. I knew I could not dare ask by parents for money, as I had watched my older siblings getting their hustles on if they needed funds for additional after-school activities. I had to hustle, as I went raking leaves, running errands, and offering to take out the trash for a few elderly neighbors. I was immensely proud of the fact that after hand-me-downs, and more hand-me-downs, I was only a few days away from getting my first-ever brand-new pair of tennis shoes.

Our ninth-grade basketball team was incredibly talented and was led by Fred Arrington, Mike Muff, and Ray Causey. Losing only one game the entire season, we could not wait to get revenge against our lone defeat in the tournament, Weisser Park. After we both finished our last regular season games with blow-out wins, we found out that they we would meet those same two teams we had just demolished in the first round of the tournament. We all were so fired up and could not wait to get to our second-round matchup. But then the unthinkable happened: the same team we had just beaten by 25 or 30 points upset us in the very first round. We were devastated! We were even more upset thinking that the team we disliked the most was on its way to winning the city championship. Little did we know that the team was being upset at the same exact time. What I tough way to learn some tough life lessons: respecting your opponents, keeping mental toughness, and never taking anything or anyone for granted.

A huge shout-out to two of my all-time favorite teachers: Betty Stein (RIP) and Janet Browser (RIP). They both had taught all my older siblings, and they both held me to the standard that my siblings had set before me. They both encouraged me daily and planted the vision of serving, participating in the community, and making a difference in other people's lives. In am eternally grateful for every minute at Fairfield Middle School.

CHAPTER 5

Seeds of Greatness

AS MEMBERS OF TEAM JORDAN, THROUGHOUT our entire childhood, my parents always found subtle ways to send strong, direct, and tough love seeds of greatness to each of us. These strong lessons included those of working hard, caring for others, playing as a team, being strong, serving God, maintaining high expectations, practicing gratitude, making no excuses, and not ever being concerned about what anyone outside of the Jordan household thought of us.

My mama always seemed to be the ultimate team player, as every time she would see or hear that St. John Missionary Baptist Church, Hanna Elementary School, Fairfield Middle School, or any of our neighbors needed help or bodies for anything, we were assigned. None of these events ever warranted any kind of discussion. It was a done deal.

With twelve mouths to feed, the words "leftovers" and "extra" were not things that applied to our household. Having only one car (with Pops working two jobs), walking all of us to Wednesday Bible study and Sunday church service every week was a given. Our oldest brother Will had the responsibility of cutting all the boys' hair (he was bad). We all had to participate in Vacation Bible School, Easter, and Christmas presentations at church every year, singing in the choirs (church and school), playing instruments, and reciting speeches and poems. When our childhood Pastor James Bledsoe (RIP) announced that he was looking for young men twelve and older to help St. John Missionary Baptist to build our new church building, we knew that the Jordan boys would have to work from dusk to dawn for two dollars a day. We were not happy, because there went our summer!

Early on, we witnessed and knew that the grind was real. We all understood that if we needed money to participate in after-school activities or sports, we had to make it happen. My older brothers always had morning and evening paper routes. We had regular customers for whom we would shovel snow, make store runs, take trash out, cut grass with a push lawnmower, collect pop (soda) bottles, wash cars (Mike's Car Wash), paint houses, cut weeds for neighborhood businesses, do construction work (Gaines family business)—whatever we needed to do. Many times, we knew that if one of us had a job to do, Mama would recruit a couple of us to join in. Brother Charles quickly learned and became the master of the wealth principle of incorporating the efforts of others.

On top of those things, we all were assigned daily chores. My main job was making sure that the kitchen floor was mopped and clean every night before I went to bed. If I forgot to do it or if Mama thought it was not done well enough, I would be awakened early the next morning (cold, hot, tired) and to mop it again (many times crying, with no shoes on, in my underwear). We were expected to be clean and always do our best.

Being the fourth boy, I was the recipient of hand-me, hand-me, and hand-me-downs, as I was always awarded my three older brothers' clothes once they outgrew them or got tired of them. In fact, I do not remember getting my first pair of new tennis shoes (Chuck Taylors, our Nikes) until my freshman year in middle school. This pattern would follow me throughout my entire high school career. I looked up to my brothers so much that I was honored to be able to wear their stuff. You could not have told me otherwise.

TEAM JORDAN

Team Jordan was blessed to never had to go outside of my house to find our mentors, hero's or to feel loved! You see, at an early age (thirteen) I found out that I loved being part of a team! But my entire life changed when I realized the magic, dynamics, possibilities, and power that came with being a part of one! My family has always been my security blanket, as there was never a day where I didn't feel love. Team Jordan would always provide each of us the foundation on how to live, love, have faith, and win!

Deeply engraved in each of us that no one ever wins or creates success alone! Everyone needs to have folk by their side who truly care about, encourages, support, and loves them. I would quickly learn that I would not, could not ever accomplish anything alone! This premise would serve as the foundation of everything I touched and/or was blessed to experience and accomplish in my life!

I reflect on my early childhood often. And I am always led back to those precious memories; that of being so blessed to be a part of this powerful team, Team Jordan. My parents, Willie James Jordan (RIP Pops), and Laura Mae Jordan, both of who did not finish high school, were among the most caring, loving, and wisest people I have ever known. To raise ten God-fearing and positive kids in a cruel, negative, and judgmental world is truly amazing! Though I lost Mama when I was seventeen, my mom was simply the gold star standard of serving God, unshaken faith, motherhood, strength, beauty, family, love, trust, loyalty, and integrity!

My hardworking Pops was willing and would do anything to keep a roof over his family's head. He made sure we had food, shelter, and the best life he could give us. Many times, going to jobs that did not treat him like the man he was, or what he deserved! Most of the time working two jobs to make sure we had what we needed. Pops toughness, magnetic personality, and wisdom were off the charts! He could make a powerful statement (a few words), did not wait to hear what you had to say, and would just walk anyway. Pops watched his favorite tv show Stanford & Sons every night before he went to bed. I am sure that he is the reason why still to this day, we have our own Jordan comedy show every time we get together! There was nothing like it! Many times, the million-dollar nuggets and advice he gave was so profound that sometimes we would just look at each other, smile, and wouldn't get it until minutes later. I still remember many of them today!

One of my favorites, most powerful and profound Pops nuggets was when after a game one of my brothers came home complaining to all of us about how one of his teammates had lost the game because he missed a free throw... WHAT! My dad overheard the conversation, walked in and as loud and as forceful as he could he said...OHHHH so you mean to tell me that you played a perfect game, made all of your shots, made no mistakes, and HAD NOTHING TO DO with that lose! WOW! And of course, the walk away, not caring to hear whatever excuse anyone could have come up with! BAM! Twenty-second-lifetime nuggets!

My amazing sisters, Suzette, Diana, and Laurietta are all so dear. They are all different, but each God-fearing, special, beautiful (inside and out), amazing parents and wives! All three are truly vested in their faith, serving their church homes and communities, and have been there for me during some of the most difficult times of my life! Team Jordan, thank God, and is so grateful that the good Lord has granted each of them with God-fearing, awesome husbands (Richard Phillips, David Martin, and Pastor Glenn Faulkner).

My phenomenal brothers, Willie, Charles, Lafayette, Douglas, Art, and Joe, have all been blessed with many different gifts and skills! But they all share the same love for God. They all have servant's hearts, a sense of community, commitment to family, are awesome fathers and each possesses compassion for others! It's literally impossible for anyone to break the bond, respect, and love for each other more. For well over sixty years now the stories, the respect, the laughs, the tears, tough truths, and the love has never wavered...oh and did I say laughter!

My older brother Willie was as solid and consistent as you would ever want or need a Big Brother to be. Talented and gifted, he set the table of expectation for all his brothers. Early on his determination for a better life, love of family, leadership, and compassion fueled fire inside each of us. Looking back, I still don't know how he did this; imagine getting married in college to your high school sweetheart, she becomes pregnant (with beautiful twins), while both working and going to school full time. Knowing that either of their parents was not in a position to help, and he had to maintain a certain class load and GPA to stay in school, all without complaining. In fact, I do not think that I have ever heard him complain about anything! WOW!

Willie would go on to teach school at an inner-city Geyer middle school (there is that word consistency again). For close to thirty-five years before retiring, he remains heavily involved with youth in the city whether they were involved in the school system or not. To say that he impacted and made a difference in thousands of kids' lives is a grave understatement.

My beautiful sisters Suzette and Diane were always classy ladies (in every sense of the word). Both loving, nurturing, loved getting dolled up (smile), helping others, and extremely talented and creative. Suzette's golden voice constantly lights up the house, and she loves interior decorating. While sweetheart of a sister, Diane had mad seamstress skills and was clearly the best cook in the house, it did not take us long to learn that her cooking secret was that she did it with love!

When I think of my big brother Lafayette, I think about his toughest, determination, tenaciousness, competitiveness, and willingness to work his tail end off! Forever the enforcer of the family, the neighborhood bullies would not say a word when Lafayette was around! He could beat up the house, but wouldn't allow anyone to touch his siblings, he just didn't play that! No matter what we were playing, he was going to do whatever it took to win! As a teenager, I hated playing one-on-one with him. As I got older, I realized that those times made me stronger, tougher, and better! As a family, we were blessed to see him overcome some tremendous challenges to become an amazing father, husband, brother, uncle, granddad, man of God, community leader, and friend to many!

My three younger brothers Doug, Art, and Joe! WOW! It seems like yesterday when they were kicking down walls in our bedroom playing sock and hanger basketball, running over to Hanna elementary to play tackle football with all the neighborhood kids, fighting and playing electric football games, one-on-one/two-on-two basketball games, racing each other in sprints on our street or around the entire block! They learned and loved to compete and hated to lose. As massive teasing (and sometimes fights) would happen regularly! Douglas the oldest of the three was an incredible athlete, he could throw a football perfectly from sixty yards away, extremely strong physically he would go days playing neighborhood football games without getting tackled. Unfortunately, he came along when it was taboo to even entertain the thought of having a black high school quarterback in the seventies. Douglas would go on to father six beautiful children and a long career in the workforce. I learned to admire his passion, work ethic, consistency, commitment to his faith, and accomplishments!

My brother Art was concerned about the quiet one, as everyone outside of our household always thought that he was who he was. His outward appearance did not match that fire to win that was burning inside! He had the keen ability to draw people to him, as he has always been a people magnet. He would go on the use those great skills to find his passion and success, as he would be one of the top salesmen in every company that was fortunate enough to have him. He too was a great athlete, as he too loved the game of basketball, as he was probably the best shooter in the Jordan household. He would go on to play college basketball, but he is most respected for the fact that he is a tremendous dad, husband, man of God, brother, uncle, and man. His crown jewels are his beautiful wife, Jeanie (thirty-plus years), and his awesome children.

My little brother Joe was by far the worse loser of the three, and even though he was very thin he somehow found a way to get himself involved in many fights. But I think he knew that big brother Douglas was not going to be too far away! Joe was a complete sponge, as he would soar up all the information, and knowledge he could. Joe showed crazy toughness, heart, and leadership skills at an early age, as his Jefferson middle school football, basketball, and track teams never lost a game or meet in three years! After a short stint in college (Texas) he was homesick and decided to return home a get a job. A short time later he was given another opportunity with hometown college Indiana Tech, to say he made the most of it is an understatement. He would go on to become a NAIA All-American, a Hall of Fame Player, earned his bachelor's and master's degrees. He was recently named Indiana Executive of the Year. As Executive Director of the Boys and Girls Club (Fort Wayne, IN) Joe recently raised fifteen million dollars to open a brand-new state-of-the-art facility for his kids and the community. The essence of community service, determination, leadership, vision and bounce back!

CHAPTER 6

Compete

IN THE JORDAN HOUSEHOLD, IT WAS an unspoken expectation that each of us had no choice but to strive to be our best selves. As a child, I was in awe of all the academic ribbons and certificates, scholastic achievements, athletic accolades, and service recognitions that my older siblings received every year. The toughest part was that they all set an extremely high bar for me and my three younger brothers Joe, Art, and Doug. No pressure!

It was tough being a year behind my sister Laurietta in school, as she was not only an awesome basketball player, but also a brilliant student. Not only that, but everybody (including the teachers) seemed to love her. Plus, her competitive spirit was off the charts. Out of love and motivation, she teased me a lot.

As luck would have it, I always got the same teachers Laurietta had the following year. So I made sure that I gave my public service announcement to each teacher the very first week of school. "Are you Laurietta's brother?"

"Yes, ma'am [or sir], I am, but please know that I am NOT Laurietta!" The entire class usually broke out in laughter.

You see, for some strange reason, all my older siblings excelled in the classroom, which seemed to come easily for them. For me, not so much. I had to work hard to maintain a B-minus average; if not, I was not going to be able to participate in any after-school activities.

We were so blessed to never have to worry about not having to go outside of our household to try to find someone to play games or sports with. Electric football tournaments, neighbor tackle football, kick ball, dodge ball (backyard, parks, schools), baseball, one-on-one games, two-on-two, three-on-three, block track races, boxing, and any other competition we could find or make up. The loser(s) always seemed to get teased and wanted a do over. It was an unspoken rule in the Jordan household that if you were not trying to win, then do not play.

To this day, I am still not sure who were the worst—my three younger brothers, Doug, Art, and Joe; my three older brothers, Willie, Charles, and Lafayette; or me. It seems like yesterday when my younger brothers were upstairs kicking down our bedroom wall playing sock and hanger basketball, running over to Hanna Elementary to play tackle football with all the neighborhood kids, fighting and playing electric football games, one-on-one/two-on-two basketball games, or racing each other in sprints on our street or around the entire block. They learned and loved to compete and hated to lose. Massive teasing (and sometimes fights) would happen regularly.

Douglas, the third youngest in our family, was an incredible athlete; he could throw a football perfectly from sixty yards away. Extremely strong physically, he would go days playing neighborhood football games without getting tackled. My brother Art was considered the quiet one, but his outward appearance did not match the fire to win that was burning inside of him—he was undoubtedly the best jump shooter in the house. While brother Joe was by far the worst loser of the three, and even though he was very thin, he always competed as if he were the toughest dog in the fight. Early on we could all see their crazy toughness, heart, passion, work ethic, compassion, winning attitudes, and leadership skills. They would never disappoint, as they each would go onto to be amazing fathers and community leaders, and they would achieve and excel at high levels.

I smile when I look back on the different ways my older brothers would try to get into my head, make me tougher, and motivate me—most were not nice. Many times I would cry when they would not let me go to the hoop with them, because I was not yet good enough to play with them. To this day I am not sure if they knew that I just wanted to go watch and be around them.

They would get tired of my asking to go with them, so one day, when I was age thirteen, my favorite Uncle John and my brothers loaded up Willie's car to go off to find the best hoops happening in the city that day. They finally said yes! "OK, we need you to run to the backyard and grab the basketball." I took off running as fast as I could. When I returned, of course with no ball, they were gone. My heart was broken. We could not be thin-skinned in the Jordan household. I did not sleep well that night. Once they starting to see my insane passion, hunger, and work, they were all in. I knew things were changing when one day out of nowhere, they decided to let me jump into the car with them. I was jacked!

Fifty years later, we still laugh about those days. Today I am so grateful for their insights, nuggets, tough love, transparency, and inspiration along my journey. The crazy thing is that each one of them has lived a full, amazing, impactful, and rewarding life, each worthy of writing his own book. I am extremely grateful and blessed. Thank you, Lord!

CHAPTER 7

Dreaming of Being a Tiger

LITTLE DID RAY AND I KNOW that this would be the last time we would ever be teammates again. We thought we had it all mapped out. We were going to go to Central High School, becoming like all our Tiger heroes (my brother Lafayette was a starting center for one of those great teams); we were going to win a state championship and do some amazing things together. We loved those Central Tigers. We would listen to all the football and basketball games that were broadcast on the radio. We would get in trouble for leaving our middle school practices and walking to Central to sneak into their JV games early so we could see our Tigers play. We could name all the Central High star athletes that played any sport, we would try to emulate their games, and we would call out their names when we were playing one on one.

Near the end of our freshman year (while still in middle school), we got some crushing news. First, we found out that they were closing Central High School and we were going to be bused miles away out of our neighborhood. Then we found out that the Causeys were moving down south, and Ray would be attending a brand-new school (Wayne High). Thirdly, I would be bused out north to Wayne's brand-new twin, Northrop High School. Needless to say, thousands of families were not happy. Many of the people did not want us at the new school, and we did not want to be there. Everything Ray and I had talked about, envisioned, and dreamed about was gone. I remember both of us crying and trying to figure what we could do, as if we had some say in the matter.

Over the summer, Ray and I found ways to get together at least three to four times a week to meet at one of our favorite outdoor basketball courts. But we both knew that changes were coming. Being as competitive as we both were, we knew that we had to start preparing for the new normality of our journey of not being teammates, not getting to be Central Tigers, and not seeing each other every day. Ray was a huge dreamer and always had big vision. I knew things had changed when he started saying things like "Wayne was going to win city" or "Wayne was going to win state." Of course, I had to respond. I found myself expanding my vision, dreams, and work ethic even more. I now realize that my best friend had quickly become a rival, and knowing Ray, he was going to work his butt off to achieve everything he wanted. I would later find out just how valuable those moments with him helped me grow.

My sidekick was gone, my older brothers were in college and out of the house, and I was praying for someone with which to vent and to hang out. So I started to form a special friendship with my neighbor Larry Hamilton, who lived two houses down from us. Larry's sister Edna was a classmate of mine, and Larry was two years older than we were. He was a successful high school football player who I could easily talk to. I had easy access to Larry because the Hamiltons lived only two houses down from us. He became a huge blessing for me, as he would allow me to hang out on his front porch many nights to chat about life, football, sports, and everything. After being a Tiger, Larry would also be attending Northrop High School for his senior year. It did give me a level of comfort knowing that. I could not wait to watch him and my good friend Fred Arrington play football that fall.

Spending time with Larry and having those competitive and challenging conversations with Raymond, I found myself getting excited about being a Northrop Bruin. So, for some strange reason, I volunteered to be a student manager for the football team prior to the school doors officially opening. My first thought was that I had found a way to get in all the games free and to travel with the team. I was jacked!

Our football team started its first-ever practices at Northwood Middle School because Northrop's football field was not ready quite yet. So every day, at the start and end of each practice, we would move the all the balls, pads, and football equipment from storage and load the station wagon owned by our senior manager, Scott. One day, Scott asked me to get behind the wheel, at which time my pride took over. I was not willing to admit that I could not drive and had never been behind the wheel of a car in my life. As you can imagine, things did not turn out too well. While backing up to the storage area, I hit the building and damaged Scott's car. To say that I was scared would be a huge understatement. I did not know who to call, but I knew that calling Mama or Pops was not an option. I decided to call my big brother Willie. And he was amazing. Willie told me to calm down and relax, and he assured me that "WE will get through it." To this day, I am not sure what happened or what he said to Scott (after I handed him the phone), but it was done. Once again, he was my hero, who I still have never seen sweat or complain about anything. To say that I started my high school career with a bang would be correct.

I soon discovered that many of the same staff and teachers from Central High School who had taught all my siblings and many of my relatives were moving to Northrop High School as well. It didn't take long for me to realize the legacy they had left for me, as the new staff informed my mom that I was selected to be one of the few incoming (diverse) group of sophomore students to be a part of a leadership planning and strategic committee. Some of their goals were to come up with ideas and activities that could possibly ease the anticipated racial tension that we all knew that this busing decision was going to cause. Of course, I did not get to choose whether I was going to accept or not. At our first meeting, I was thinking that I had never seen so many white folks in my life. I had decided that this was not going to be Central, but it was the next best thing. As Team Jordan would always say, it is all about what you believe.

CHAPTER 8

Imbued with Her Spirit—Mama

I'M NOT SURE WHERE TO BEGIN. I have been tremendously blessed to have traveled the world and to have met some incredible human beings. But I thank God every day for letting me be the son of the strongest, most loyal, most faithful, most loving, most nurturing, and most selfless person I have ever met.

As a child, I would sometimes watch my mother walk through a neighbor's yard to get to work. We could literally see the laundry company (American Linen Company) where she worked from our front porch. Before she headed to her job every morning, she would get up at the break of dawn to give us something to eat, fix our lunch bags, and make sure we had clean clothes for school. Most times during the spring and summer months, American Linen Company would keep their delivery door open to help with circulation for their electric fans (no air conditioning), and we could see Mama and her co-workers standing on their feet for eight hours on a concrete floor. Sometimes temperatures in the laundry company would reach 100-plus degrees.

Every day, after arriving home and before she started dinner, Mama would first check on all her children, making sure that we were all right and that we had our homework and chores done. We never once saw her complain or think about herself. As my sister Diane got older, she would help Mama with the cooking.

Once we arrived home from school, we were always eager to find something to snack on. Most of the times when we searched the kitchen for food, we found nothing. We would always wonder how all of us could be looking everywhere and not find a thing, whereas Mama would come home, look at that same empty pantry, and find enough to feed her entire family.

One day we asked my brother Charles to explain that to us. He responded, "You see, we all went to the pantry looking to feed ourselves, while Mama went to the pantry looking to feed somebody else, so she had help called the Holy Spirit."

Mom would say, "You all were so blinded by greed that you couldn't even see the food right in front of you."

There had to be something to that, as we all knew that Mama did not play, but she ruled with an iron fist. It seemed that she had the incredible ability to know stuff that we had thought we'd gotten away with or that she would never find out. Her strong morals, values, and unwavering faith were not to be tested or challenged. In the Jordan household, we were going to serve the Lord, respect grown folk, treat everybody right, love one another, work our butts off, and be the best people we could be. On top of that, she made sure that we were strong and had the ability to stand up for ourselves.

When I was in third or fourth grade, the latter became crystal clear to all of us. One night our neighborhood Hanna Elementary School was having its weekly Recreation Night

School, where the neighbor kids could go to play games, socialize, and have fun. While my beautiful and oldest sister, Suezette was there, a girl tried to pick a fight with her over a boy that Suzette didn't even like. Suezette, knowing and being fearful of Mama and Pops, did everything she could to avoid that fight. The girl would not take no for an answer, as she proceeded to follow and escort Suezette all the way to our front door. Of course, the noisy instigating group of kids followed. As Suezette tearfully came inside of the house, my mom asked what was going on. My sister told Mama that this girl had followed her home and wanted to fight her over some boy, and she didn't want to get in trouble, so she didn't. That was the first time I ever saw Mama that angry. She responded, "She's in your front yard and wants to fight you. Okay, you'd better go out there and kick her butt!" Suezette proceeded to do just that. The beat down wasn't pretty, but the message sent to our community, and to all of us, was loud and clear. I am sure that my sisters Suezette, Diane, and Laurietta were good from that day forward. As always, Mama knew exactly what she was doing.

I must admit that when it came time for me to get to a basketball court and hoop, I was a tad bit hard-headed. I missed many curfews because basketball had become my first and only love, and I had to find a way to get on the court. I will never forget the Wednesday when I knew Mama and Aunt Carrie would be walking to church for Bible study. On this night, I was not supposed to leave the house because I was on punishment. But all day in school, the fellas were all talking about hooping at six o'clock, and I had to be there. I was running late, so as I watched them turn the corner, I took off though the back door. But I did not get very far, as I was promptly hit by a car in our back alley. My first thoughts were of my mother and the trouble

I was going to be in. That fear somehow enabled me to get up and run into the house with the driver chasing me to find out if I was okay. One of my brothers then ran to catch up to my mom and aunt to let them know that I had just been hit by a car. I would find out that I had a broken arm, but all I could think of was the butt kicking and huge punishment (no hoops) I was going to get.

As we became adults, most of us would share stories about how Mama would hold on to stuff that we all thought we had gotten away with until she had enough energy and felt that we really needed to have a butt-whooping. It was during those times that she would call out all the things that we thought we had gotten away with. She was not a big woman, and we were always amazed by her brute strength and her ability to hold each of us with one hand and whoop a behind with the other. As we got older, we finally figured out that she had some special help.

One of the most amazing things about my mom was her unwavering, unapologetic faith and commitment to her Lord and Savior Jesus Christ. Every night like clock-work, she would be upstairs on her knees in her bedroom praying out loud. It did not matter what was going on around her; Mama was in her zone. The only thing that mattered to her at that time was spending time with the Lord. No matter what, every night for what seemed like hours, we could hear her throughout the house praising, honoring, edifying, and lifting the Lord in prayer. Every night she would not get up until she had prayed for Pops and each of her children individually by name.

My mom's natural living journey of walking in faith, not fear, was on display her entire life. She taught each of us to know right from wrong, and to make sure that when we saw something that was not right, we had a responsibility and duty to stand up and speak up. She taught us to be more concerned with doing what we knew was right than being right, regardless of what anyone else thought or said.

She was the epitome of motherhood, faith, strength, beauty, family, love, trust, loyalty, selflessness, and integrity. My siblings and I could only conclude that we rose because we were imbued with this spirit of our mother, Laura Mae Jordan. Her spirit transcends time, space, and distance. That is the reason why we can live hundreds of miles apart, and when we do get to speak to or see each other, no distance or time has separated us. It is like we are still in our home at 312 E. Masterson Street.

CHAPTER 9

Remember the Bruins!

GROWING UP IN OUR NEIGHBORHOOD, MOST of us loved (and played) all sports, with basketball and football at the top of the list. Knowing that I was going through a serious growth spurt, while weighing 130 pounds dripping wet, I knew that playing football was not in the cards. I had so much respect for Fred Arrington and Larry Hamilton that I knew I wanted to find a way to be around them, so prior to the start of the school year, I volunteered to be a manager on the football team. I knew with Larry living only three houses down, I would be able to ride to and from practices with him. Plus, I would get to get to see all the games for free, which seemed to be a surprisingly good deal. Remember, I was a Jordan, and the thought of what other folk thought of me never once entered my mind. It was the very first time I had ever experienced being the minority on a sports team, let alone in a school environment.

Little did I know that it was preparing me for the unknowns with the very first day of nationwide busing only days away. I did not quite get it yet, as my mom sat us all down for our usual first day of school conversation about what she expected from all of us the upcoming school year. But for some reason, we all noticed that this conversation and message carried a different tone. She laid down the law about being leaders, not following the crowd, making smart decisions, and understanding who we were and whose we were. As always, "I had better not ever have to leave my job to come up to that school!" We had no idea that our first day of school would be one for the history books.

It was 1971, and none of us had a clue. As many of my neighbors, classmates, friends, and teammates from Fairfield Middle School and I loaded the bus, we could feel the tension, the fear of the unknown, and not knowing what to expect once we arrived. As we passed at least four other high schools closer to our homes en route to Northrop, many of us were still not comfortable with the fact that they had closed our dream school, as we all wanted to follow in our older siblings' footsteps and become Tigers.

I did take a little bit of comfort in knowing that many of our new school's staff members were former Central High School teachers. The closer the bus got to the high school, the more nervous I became. A few of my friends and I huddled up together to enter the building. We had been given maps and information to our homerooms where we all needed to report. The staff members were warm and very welcoming, so I was beginning to feel a little better—but it did not last long. Soon afterward, a series of fights took place near the main entrance, cafeteria, and the gymnasium. Several groups of individuals had bought chains, sticks, and other items as weapons; kids were thrown through the windows and against the walls and were beaten. The racial tension was intense and insane. Some people did not want us there, and many of us did not want to be there. If there were no police officers on duty, it would have been even crazier.

Several arrests were made, but it still did not seem to calm the masses. For the next several weeks, the students (both black and white) who were expelled would attempt to sneak into the school at lunch time or after school to finish what they had started. I remember thinking, How are we are ever going to get through this? I keep hearing my mom's voice, "Treat everybody as if they were worth a million dollars, any if they are worth a penny." What I knew for sure was that I had better never entertain getting involved in this mess as I was more afraid of my parents than anyone at school.

Being a manager of the football team suddenly came with huge benefits. Over a four-week period, I had been blessed to witness firsthand how a group of talented and gifted football players who had competed against each other in PAL (Police Athletic Leagues) in middle school, did not look like each other, and probably weren't happy about this busing deal, had started to laugh, enjoy each other, fight like brothers, and became friends and teammates. The team was under the guidance of Hall of Fame Coach Buzz Doerfler, who had been a builder of men and was a winner his entire life. It was blessed with tremendous senior leaders, including my friend Larry Hamilton and others. Best of all, it was led by all-everything George McCowan. Not only did George look like me, but he was also an outstanding football player, a great wrestler, a track performer, an exceptional student-athlete, and a better person. He was respected and loved by everyone. I could not help but be in awe and take notes.

With all this drama going on, I reflected on the messages, nuggets, directives, expectations, and player/team bonding activities that Coach Doerfler and his awesome staff gave to the players. It appeared that their goal was to simply erase ignorance, fear, and not knowing what to expect from each other. Of course, I was a sponge.

Behind the scenes, our fall sports teams were in full execution mode. Our cross-country team, led by future Hall of Fame Coach Barrie Peterson and all-everything senior Rick "Die Hard" Magley, had been preparing to take the city and the state by storm. From day one, drama, cheerleading tryouts, cheer block, marching band practices, and many other activities took place. We were off and running!

The challenges of bonding and becoming a team in every arena were going to be a huge undertaking for our coaches, administration, and student body. As I sat back and embraced the fact that at the end of every school day, I was blessed to be in this football team environment where I saw that classmates and teammates had found a way to start to jell together, fight together, and root for each other. I could not wait until our first-ever Friday Night Lights football game. Slowly but surely, I could see, as the coach would say, "Leaders show up!"

Our cross-country and football teams would go on to shock the entire city with their immediate success. It would be the beginning of slowly giving all of us a common theme to build on. We were Bruins! They had set the example, the team spirit, and the high expectations for all future Bruins teams and players. Many of those great senior athletes played multiple sports including tennis, baseball, wrestling, and track. Many of them would be the first Bruins to go on to college to perform at the next level. City, sectional, and regional championship trophies were starting to fill an empty school trophy case.

At that time, I discovered that I had already been a part of two teams, Team Jordan and the Fairfield Spartans hoop team. It was during those times when I realized that I loved being part of a team. A year or so later, at age sixteen, I figured out that I was way below average by myself, but with the right team, teammates, coaches (mentors), and mindset, I could be special. I felt as if I had found my secret sauce!

By this time, I had grown three inches in one year. At basketball tryouts, I had told myself that I was going to work harder than anyone else. My confidence was as high as it had ever been, as I knew that I had to work by butt off, and my brother Charles had really helped me improve my mental toughness, IQ, ball handling, shooting, and confidence. But he was not anticipating that I would grow four inches while he was in school at Indiana. I would call him and say, "Guess what, I'm six feet tall now!" "Yeah, right!" A few months later, "Guess what, I'm six foot two now!" "Yeah, right!" "Hey, bruh, I'm six foot three now!" "Yeah, right!"

Things seemed to be falling into place, as I was blessed to have a coach, Dan Howe, who saw promise in this razor-thin kid whose body was all over the place and growing like a weed. I would soon find out that several of my sophomore classmates were already elevated to the junior varsity and varsity teams before tryouts were ever held. As our season progressed, our varsity team was struggling as we had great skilled premier players but no post presence. At the time, my middle school classmate, teammate, and good friend Mike Muff was already six feet, four inches tall and a beast of a man, and he was developing into a fairly good player. Halfway through the season, the varsity coach, Bob Dillie, decided to move Mike up to the varsity team. A few days later, not only was Mike on the varsity team, but he was also in the starting lineup! The weekend slate of games included a Friday road game against Concordia and a Saturday home game against Huntington North, two strong opponents.

My guy Mike, who I would ride with to the JV games, sat together watching, dreaming about, and talking about how excited we were about getting our chance to play on that big stage—and it was now here! Mind you, Mike was not the first or second leading scorer on junior varsity team, but everybody knew that he was destined to be an amazing player. In his first-ever varsity game, Mike quickly served noticed by scoring 22 points and grabbing 10 rebounds in a huge road victory for the Bruins. He then followed up the next night by scoring 20 points and grabbing 9 boards in another victory, earning him the SAC (Summit Athletic Conference) Player of the Week. He was now on the map!

Mike's personality was always warm, fun, jovial, and welcoming. He was a great teammate, friend, and good person. But in school the following week, I watched how everyone seemed to treat Mike differently. People who previously would not speak to him were now all over him. Of course, he had a new set of teammates and a new circle of friends. His cool status had exploded seemingly over-night. Even though it meant less time for us, I was genu-inely happy for him. Once again, I was told by Team Jordan that I had to work harder, get tougher, get better, and fight for what I wanted. I was reminded to always keep the main thing the main thing, and that whatever the good Lord had for me, he had for only me, and that there will never be any free lunches. I was super thrilled for my brother Mike. I had become a proud Bruin and cheered on our varsity team as if I were in the game. To say I was proud, inspired, and fired up could not adequately explain what I was feeling.

I would go on to play on both the C Team (sopho-more team) and junior varsity, as a few of my classmates thought it was beneath them to play on the C Team. I was jacked, as I learned that I could sometimes play three to four games a week (eligible to play up to five total quarters between both). I am so grateful that both the C Team Coach Ormerod and JV Coach Howe saw something and expressed so much confidence in me. Splitting practice times between the two, I was in heaven, until I realized that our varsity team the next season would be returning at least ten seniors, and all our junior varsity team would be fighting for spots as well. The odds for sure seem to be stacked against me. Nevertheless, my confidence was though the roof, and I could not wait to put the work in.

It was around this time when I started to have serious dreams about achieving massive success on the court, listening to college games and stars (Rick Mount, Austin Carr, and Pistol Pete Maravich) on the radio, dreaming about being six feet, eight inches tall, and disappearing to hoop every chance I got. I knew a whooping was coming, but I didn't worry about 'em until I was on my way home. I thought Mom would get tired one day. She never did, though. Despite the challenges, I had fallen in love with my classmates, teammates, and coaches, and I was proud of being a Bruin.

Raymond Causey and I were so excited about the last day of school, as we would talk on the phone about our vision for our different teams, whose team was going to win city and state, and who were the best players in the city in our class and in the upper classes. Of course, my name never came up.

One Wednesday night during the basketball season, we decided to meet up and walk a few miles to Concordia High School to watch a guy named Eugene Parker play. I had heard about how great of a player he was for at least two years. He played in the Lutheran private school circuit and did not attend public school. He was in our class and without question was one of the best players in the city, even as a sophomore. He did not disappoint, as he was head and shoulders above anybody I had seen in our class. A deadly left-handed shooter, he was a leader who carried himself with class and style, and he played extremely hard. I had heard that he was a gym rat and lived with a basketball in his hand. On the way home, all we could talk about was the show that Eugene had put on and just how much work we had in front of us. Run or compete was the question we asked each other. We laughed, and without saying a word, we knew the answer and what we needed to do.

I had decided that over the summer I would have zero time for anything but hoops; nothing else would matter. It also had become obvious to my three older brothers—Willie, Charles, Lafayette—and to my parents that I was all in and was willing to do whatever it took, no matter what, to achieve my goals. They had instilled in me the values, principles, and seeds of greatness, and now it was time to back me up. By brothers, who were no longer sneaking out to play ball (and they played a lot and everywhere), engaged me in many tough (no blood) one-on-one, two-on-two, three-on-three, four-on-four, and five-on-five games. Charles and I would drive to find empty courts so he could work with me on my footwork, ball handling, defense, and shooting, sometimes for hours in the scorching heat. As the best player in the family, he understood the fundamentals of the game as well as anyone, but more importantly, he knew what to say and the buttons to push to make me to go harder, do more, and be better.

A major blessing happened that summer when Willie and Charles, who were students at Indiana University (along with my sister Laurietta), decided to take me back to Bloomington for a month to hang out, work out, and be with them. They knew that I was extremely low maintenance. If they needed to keep me busy while they went to class, were at work, or had other things to do, they just had to give me a ball and drop me off at the Hyper Building (basketball courts for the students). It quickly became my heaven as every morning, afternoon, and evening, I honed my skills when no one was there. I also played against former high school athletes, a few college athletes, and my brothers' strong circle of friends. When I would show up to the apartment, it was to take a quick nap or get something to eat. They knew and encouraged my routine. It seemed as if everyone knew, loved, and respected my siblings. Charles was the first ever walk-on player for Bobby Knight and was also respected by IU greats George McGinnis, Steve Downing, and others. I was given immediate love and respect because of them.

Being in Bloomington, Indiana, in the early seventies was also educational. Like everywhere else in the North, racial tension, incidents, and racism were evident. I watched how my siblings handled things and how others on campus leaned on and looked to them for advice and guidance. On top of that, I witnessed their work ethic and determination, but just as importantly, I saw the insane amount of serious fun and laugher they were having in college. Their leadership skills and the positive effect they had on others were off the charts. Little did they know that the tough love conversations and the time spent we spent together in Bloomington gave me a clearer picture of who I was, changed my life, expanded my goals and dreams, let me know that I too was worthy, and made me hungrier than ever to win. I could not wait to get to college—by any means necessary.

Once I arrived home, our 1973 school year was upon us. I was no longer manager of the football team, but I was just as excited as if I were still there. The year before,

I had been blown away by our cross-county and track star Rick Magley's insane workout routine, as he would run five miles to school every morning, no matter what the weather; participate in an extremely challenging practice; and then after practice run back to his home. Our football (7–3 and SAC runners up), tennis, wrestling (11–3), track (SAC and sectional champs), and baseball (sectional and regional champs) teams were loaded with studs, had great coaching, and excelled at a high level for only its second year in existence. The start of the school year was a lot calmer as well. Thank you, Lord!

This was the first year that I had time to participate in our pre-season basketball conditioning program. I was excited about getting to know the upperclassmen and seeing where I stacked up against them. The year before, Coach Dillie had cut a few of the best players in our school because they were seniors, as he was grooming this extraordinarily talented group for their senior season. He settled on keeping nine returning varsity lettermen, with the top seven leading scorers from the year before returning. The three juniors he selected were Mike Muff, point guard Tom Madden, and me. I knew playing time was going to be tough!

Like every year, we would tip off our season against our archrival Northside High, always tough, loaded, and extremely hard to beat, especially at their place. In front a packed house, we went on to lose 64–73. I was surprised when the coach put me in with five minutes to go in the first half. I went on to score six points and never get back in for the second half.

Up next would be one of the toughest games on our schedule, as we would face all-everything and Cincinnati commit, Jimmy Webb, and top-ranked South Bend Adams. The year before at their place, I watched from the bleachers as Mr. Webb scored forty points (it seemed like more) as they beat us badly. Now Webb and Company were heading to our home court, and no one wanted to guard him. Coach Dillie asked me if I wanted to guard Mr. Webb. I quickly responded that I would. Not knowing if he was serious or not, I just wanted an opportunity to get into the game. Afterwards, the joke around school and the locker room was that I was going to guard Jimmy Webb on Friday. The funny thing about that was that a few of my senior teammates, who had been afraid to step up, were trying to give me advice on how to guard him all week. I would only say, "If you knew how to guard him, why didn't you step up?"

While constantly talking with my big brothers, the closer we got to tip-off time, the more excited and confident I became. I was told things like, "Boy, you have played one-on-one and competed against all of us, college athletes, and grown men—you are more than ready." And their favorite: "Do whatever you believe is right!"

I arrived for the start of our JV game to an already jam-packed arena. Usually, our varsity players would all sit together behind the bench and leave at the end of the third quarter to get dressed and ready for our game. But being so nervous, scared, or excited (I could not tell which), I headed to the locker room to get dressed as soon as the JV left the locker room for their second half; it all seemed to be happening so fast. While sitting in the locker room, I decided to pray as butterflies were racing inside of me. Knowing that there was an overflow and standing-room-only crowd of over 2,000 people did not help. After a conversation with my angel (my mom) and prayer, I felt stronger and ready!

The Bruins would go on to upset Jimmy Webb and South Bend Adams 73–60. Mr. Webb would score 28 points. I would score a then-surprising and then-career high of 16 points. Just as importantly, I earned the respect our coaching staff, my classmates, and my teammates. The rest of the year, I was a starter and would be assigned to guard the best player on the opposing team, regardless of position. Our team was loaded with talented seniors Greg Beer, Larry Davis, Wid Knight, Al Wright, Carey Ehrman, sharp-shooter Mike Whitt, and of course, Mike Muff. Tom Madden and I were filling our roles and contributing any way the team needed us to. My development was happening right in front everyone.

Our team would go one to finish the season 24–3, to become SAC (city), sectional, and regional champs; semi-state runners-up (one game away from the Indiana Final Four); and ranked third in the state of Indiana. What was so special and rewarding in this (my junior) year was seeing our entire student body, cheerleaders, and athletes from all different sports come together to attend each other's games (matches and meets) to cheer for, encourage, and lift each other up. Suddenly race, religion, and politics—nothing mattered. We were all in, and we were Bruins!

At the beginning of my junior year, I had become extremely close to our athlete director's secretary, Ms. Nancy Scheinman. Every morning before the start of my day, I would stop by her office and she would provide me with a snack, fruit, or something else to eat. She probably was my biggest fan at that time. On the last day of school, I wanted to stop by her office to say goodbye for the summer. As I approached her office, I heard her talking with my coach about the expectations for next season's team. Coach expressed his fear of us losing ten seniors with only three returning varsity players. I then heard Ms. Scheinman say she was excited, as she felt that I was going to be special next year. Shortly afterward, I heard Coach say that if we had to depend on just those three, we could be in for a long season. I was crushed! With my eyes tearing up, I had to get myself together and run to jump onto my bus to get home. Sadly, I never got a chance to say goodbye to my biggest fan.

I was glad that my mentor and big brother was home from IU for summer break. As I started to vent about what happened, he was silent and didn't respond right away. Then he said this: "You basically have two choices. You can either prove him right or you can prove him wrong. You decide!" And he walked away. From pain to purpose, decision made!

I knew this was going to be the most important summer of my young life. It was so hard to believe that my last year of high school was only a few months away. I had made my decision, as nothing was going to stop me from finding a way to work on my game.

I was thrilled to find out that my brothers had already decided to give me another summer trip to Indiana University to work in secret on my game. While in Bloomington, I found out that the 1974 Indiana High School State Championship game was to be played right there in Assembly Hall. Every time we drove by Assembly Hall, I could envision our Northrop Bruins playing there on March 23, 1974 (yep, I had found out the date). I tried to share that vision with my brothers, but they were not having it. "No one had ever heard of Northrop. You lost Mike Whitt, Greg Beer, Larry Davis, and Al Wright—you guys don't have a chance!" I was not sure if they were trying to motivate me, or if they just did not believe we could do it. It was probably the latter.

CHAPTER 10

Broken Heart to Champions

ON OUR LONG BUS RIDE THE first day of school, Mike and I were talking about how excited we were about the basketball season and our senior year. We talked about all the doubters and that fact they we were going to prove everybody wrong. We didn't quite know what, but we could feel something incredibly special happening within our entire student body, our faculty, and all our sports teams. The closeness on and off the court, fields, and mats was unlike anything I had ever experienced.

The year before I had fallen into my pregame routine, as I loved to take a one-and-a-half-hour nap, wake up, and grab a snack prior to heading out to watch and support our JV team. As several of my classmates, friends, and teammates who lived a lot closer to school than I did found this out, they would invite me over to their homes for my nap. It blew me away! A favorite was one of my friends and classmates, Greg Kline, whose father just happened to be the head coach at one of our rival school (Snider). Another was a classmate, former teammate, and friend Stan Pressley. He literally lived right across the street from the school, and his wonderful mom, Ms. Pressley, worked in our school's cafeteria. She would take care of me and always showed me a little extra love.

I had started to dream bigger and my vision seemed so far away, but so clear. My challenge was to try to get my teammates and coaches to buy into it. March 23! March 23! March 23! I started to dream about our team being interviewed on Channel 33 by legendary and Hall of Fame sportscaster Mr. Hilliard Gates. This would have meant that our team had won a sectional, regional, semi-state, or state championship, and he would interview one of the star players. I had watched many of my city and statewide heroes do this during the Indiana State tournament since I was thirteen years old. I thought that would be so cool!

The year before, I had watched many of my insanely talented city-wide rivals and excellent players such as Donald Taylor, James Lindsley, Button Hill, Reggie Burt, Ron Moore, Ray Causey, Eugene Parker, Ronnie Knox, Al McGee, Julius Stephens, Larry and Raymond Reese, Reggie Burt, Kevin Howell, Julius Stephens, Jeff Hallgrem, Kerry Sanders, Scooter Rouse, Byron Cox, and Max Richardson, to name a few, had all served notice that it was going to be a war for city-wide supremacy, this our senior season. It was on!

It was two weeks before our first game, and for some odd reason I got a message at school that my dad was going to pick me up after practice. With two jobs, he never had time to do that. Being of singular focus, I did not think much of it. When I got into the car, he said that my mom wanted to see me; all I knew was that for the past few years she had been ill, in and out of the hospital, and missing work. Yet at home, despite her noticeable weight loss, Mama was still that strong, loving, firm, unwavering, faithful, and prayerful self. I hated seeing my mom in that hospital bed.

After our brief and impactful talk, my dad told me to wait in the hallway while they talked. As I walked away, I heard her say to Dad, "That boy is going to be a pro!" I would have to admit that at no point in my wildest dreams had that been on my to-do list. My "why" for wanting to have massive success had just been defined for me; over the next several years, it would sometimes bring tears to my eyes thinking about it.

It was Thanksgiving Day weekend, on November 25, when our rock, our mom, got her wings, as the good Lord called his angel home. To say that Team Jordan was devastated was an understatement. I had never experienced such pain in my life. I did not understand why God would ever let this happen. I had always believed that God would always protect and take care of one of his most loyal and faithful servants.

We were eight days from our first game against our bitter archrivals Northside, and basketball was the furthest thing from my mind. I knew that the following week was going to be insanely tough. As our large family spend time grieving, praying, and preparing for my mom's home-going celebration, I did not attend school or basketball practice.

But every day after school and practice, my teammates, our cheerleaders, and a boatload of my classmates would come by and check on me. I do not think half of them had ever been in the inner city before. Their heartfelt and overwhelming love and support were felt by not only me, but also my entire family, neighborhood, teammates, classmates, and coaches. The night before our game, my older brothers asked me how I felt, and they told me that they had been blown away by the love everyone had given me, and that Mom would have wanted me to play. That night I prayed hard for strength, as I was not sure I could pull it off.

Game day the next day, there was a serious buzz in the hallways and cafeteria about the game. Being back in that environment was exactly what I needed. Prior to the game, I was repeatedly told that Mama would be with me and to pray.

It would be the first time I could feel her presence over me. I would hit two free throws in the closing minutes to help us upset a strong, talented, and veteran Northside team. And I had found my secret sauce: prayer and my mama. The next night, we hit the road to play powerhouse South Bend Adams, who had just reached the state finals the year before. We ended up losing a hard-fought game by three points. On the bus back home, there was not a dry eye in on the bus. Mike Muff yelled out loud: "We are not losing another game this year!" We were all in! Those previous ten days would go on to change our lives forever.

We could not wait to get to practice, as our coaches worked us, made practices fun, were always positive, and loved us. We knew we had tough games ahead against some incredibly talented teams and players, including our strong SAC rivals, traditionally powerful Marion, and road games at Concordia, Huntington North, Penn, and Southside. Week after week, we would find a way to motivate each other by building up the key players on our opponents' team; it always kept us focused on what was ahead of us.

I passionately believe that our team was filled with high character individuals, leaders, good people, and proven winners. Several were star players and captains on other successful Bruin teams. The competition in our practices was always intense and physical. From the last player on our roster to the first, we held each other accountable. The coaches believed in us and never had to coach attitude or work ethic. We had a lot of love and respect for each other, and we were awfully close to our awesome cheerleaders, crazy fans, and faculty. Hundreds of them would carpool to pack out our road games, and of course, we had standing room of 2,000 or more at all of our home games. Everyone knew that I always wore my emotions on my sleeves. I would be so fired up about our team, school, and fans that I quickly earned the nickname "Cheerleader" from the media and our fans. Big things were happening!

Our first real sign of how good we could be happened on the road in front of 7,500 fans against Marion (which had the fifth largest high school gym in the world). We blew them out on their home floor. Mike Muff scored 28 points and grabbed 15 rebounds, Tom Madden controlled the tempo and dished out 17 assists, James Wimbley scored a double-double, and I scored at a Marion Giants opponent (and my career high) record 37 points. On the bus ride home, all I could think about was my secret sauce, as the entire game I could feel my mom's presence.

It was around that time when people stated to notice our team and just how good we were. Because of the noticeable passion, emotions, and enthusiasm I played with, a reporter named me "The Cheerleader"; it caught on quickly. After our huge victory, we turned our focus to winning the Summit Athletic Conference (city) Championship and finishing it undefeated. To accomplish that, we had to defeat probably the most talented team in the SAC Southside at their place. We were ready, and we soundly beat the Archers and became SAC Champs. We escaped tough road tests against superstars Eugene Parker, Ronnie Knox, and the Concordia Cadets (in the PIT), coming back from being nine points down to squeeze out a win. And then we traveled to Mishawaka, Indiana, pulling out another nail-biter in front of a sold-out hostile crowd, a very physical and talented Penn Kingsman's team, we knew that we had been battle tested.

As we entered the state tournament, we were riding high. We were full of confidence, as we knew that these new kids on the block, the Bruins, now had a huge bull's eye on our backs. Our phenomenal student body, cheerleaders, and fans had been behind us all year, and as they too had bought into the vision of being in Bloomington on March 23rd, they also loved Coach Dillie. Coach Dillie (now in his late sixties) at one of our pep rallies had stated that if we went to state, he would ride a tricycle there. The talk around town was that we were overrated and would not get out of the sectionals or regionals. Our coaches, fans, and families made sure we heard all the noise and used that to motivate us. Little did they know that we had, too. We were ready.

Each year, the Sunday afternoon prior to the start of the Indiana State tourney, WKKJ-TV 33 and my hero, Hilliard Gates, would host a statewide tournament pairing announcement show. Fort Wayne was the only city in the state that would host the Sectionals (I and II) and would tip off in the middle of the week. We would go on to win Sectional I with a 70–44 win against the Harding Hawks, a solid win versus the Woodland Warriors 75–56, and a tougher than expected 57–47 win over the Carroll Chargers. So I finally got my interview with Mr. Hilliard Gates!

After cutting down the nets and celebrating in the locker room, we rushed out to see who would win the following game and find out who we would meet in the first game of Regional play the following week. As predicted, those incredibly talented Southside Archers would be waiting for us. We could hear the buzz all around the city, as the Archers was one of the few teams that matched up with us in talent and size; many were predicting that they would defeat us in the revenge game. We jumped on them early, silencing their huge crowd and dimming their confidence early, en route to a 67–51 victory.

We were now at the stage in our journey where, after the morning game, we as a team would bus to a nearby hotel to eat, rest up, and be together. And, of course, I had my pre-game nap. We would soundly defeat the DeKalb Barons 69–48 to win our second straight Regional championship. And we had another interview with Mr. Hilliard Gates. We were loving it!

Next up was a loaded Fort Wayne semi-state. We would face the tough Logansport Berries, led by a Michigan Wolverines recruit Mark Lozier and his brother. The winner would likely take on the undefeated and number-1 ranked Anderson Indians, led by superstar dual Roy Taylor (soon to be named Indiana Mr. Basketball) and the beast Tony Marshall, who had blown us out at the same spot the year before. Getting to Bloomington was not going to be easy by any stretch.

Intense, physical, crazy, and confident were the four words that would describe our practice that Monday, until the moment one of our senior leaders, outstanding football player and tough guy Dennis Hetrick, accidentally elbowed our star Mike Muff in the eye. It was completely closed, bruised, and swollen. Mike's status for our upcoming games was now in doubt. His left eye was bloodshot red, swollen, and shut. On a call to his mom that night, I found out that his vision was blurry, he was in pain, and his doctor was not going to allow him to play if it did not clear up. As I prayed that night, I called out to my angel (my mother), once again.

The next day, while my neighborhood schoolmates and I were waiting on the school bus, we noticed that Mike was not there. Knowing what I had found out the night before, I decided not to tell anyone, especially my teammates. I knew that we had to stay positive, no matter what. In my heart of hearts, I felt strongly that we had both God and my secret weapon on our side. I believed that my boy Mike was going to be good to go.

Around lunch time, I got word that Mike was in school after going to the doctor. I could not wait to see him. Though he was not able to practice that day, the fact that he was there was enough. His presence, and his positive, jovial self, seemed to pick us all up. He and Coach Dillie had a special kind of relationship, as Coach would make us do 10–20 pushups for doing stupid stuff, but Mike could always get away with doing 5–8, counting by twos. Then Coach would laugh and say that's good. As for me, I needed to do every pushup I could. After our Wednesday and Thursday practices, with Mike going full tile, we were flooded with local and state print and television media people. After a light shoot around and walkthrough on Friday, we were confident and as ready as we could have possibly been.

In front of another sold-out Memorial Coliseum crowd, I was able to hit two big free throws to help us sneak by Logansport 55–53. Our night cap reward was a rematch with the mighty Anderson Indians. Of course, none of the sports writers, or anyone outside of our Bruin family, gave us much of a chance.

Early in the first quarter, the Indians tough guy Tony Marshall attempted that same old intimidation move he had mastered his entire career. But not this day, as our tough guy Mike Muff went chest to chest, got directly in his face, and set the tone to let everyone know in the coliseum and in our television audience that we were not going to be intimidated. The entire team sprinted to the locker room after building a halftime lead, hugging, emotional, excited, high fiving, and jumping up all over each other.

The coaches had their brief meeting outside of the locker room. They quickly found out that they could not control our emotions and did not need to discuss anything they had discussed. All they did was just smile and say, "Let's GO finish it!" We would go on to a huge upset by a score of 67–53 heard around the state. We had just shocked the entire state of Indiana!

The following week of school was just a blur as our faculty, students, and administrators had extraordinarily little interest in testing or disciplining anybody. At practice that Monday (like most practices), our awesome assistant coaches Chris Stavreti and Jim Kiem (who would later name one of his prize-winning show horses after me) always knew how to get us to relax, as they would get us to practice early so they could challenge us to a game of HORSE. It was tough to beat those old trick-shot specialists. We loved those guys! In between statewide media requests, intense practices, and team meetings, we were all busy just soaking up all the love and attention. We had already convinced ourselves that we had nothing to lose. All the pressure was now on the second, third, and fourth ranked teams in the state. We were mentally, emotionally, and physically ready to shock the state once again. On Thursday, we were told to pack for two nights, and that we needed to be prepared for a wild, crazy, exciting, and full day on Friday.

Our Friday, the school day started with homeroom for everybody. We heard over the PA the announcements of separating by graduating class whose turn was it to head to the gymnasium for the pep rally. With each tournament advancement and championship game, we had an awesome Bruin pep rally. We had no clue how huge, exciting, and crazy this one would be—a standing-room-only crowd that even included many rival players, students, and friends from other city schools. They would all be rooting for us.

After our city-wide pep rally, we loaded up our deco-
rated bus for our solid four-hour trip to Bloomington to
hundreds of excited fans. We were jacked! The drive was
smooth until we had to take I-69 and drive thru Anderson,
Indiana, as an Anderson state trooper stopped us for
speeding. We all laughed and thought that he must have
still been upset from our huge win the week before. I guess
you figured out by now that we let Coach Dillie off the
hook; he did not have to ride that tricycle.

On the agenda the rest of the day was to check into our
rooms at IU's student union and then head to Assembly
Hall for practice, then back for the team dinner, team
meeting, and lights out. We would have a dark thirty
morning wake-up call and team breakfast, and then bus over
to watch the 10 A.M. game (Jeffersonville versus Franklin),
and be ready to go. I still get chills just writing this!

March 23, 1974, was finally here, and just like that
yearlong dream, so were we. Front and center, Assembly
Hall, Bloomington, Indiana. Our alarms clocks were set for
8 A.M., as if we needed it. Mike Muff (my roommate) and
I woke up around 7:00 with our music blasting (squeezing
in my favorite theme song by the O'Jays, "For the Love of
Money"). At breakfast, we talked about leaving it all on the
floor, staying together, playing for each other, our families,
our school, and our city. To a man, we all felt that we were
prepared and ready to go.

We quickly noticed the sold-out 17,000 seat Assembly
Hall as we entered the arena. It would be the largest crowd
any of us had ever played in front of. As we settled in
to watch the first game, I found the palms of my hands
starting to sweat and my stomach filled with butterflies; I
was not sure if I was too excited or just nervous. Midway
through the first quarter, I began to pray, as I needed to
talk to God and feel the presence of my secret angel. As I

finished, I returned my attention to watching the game, knowing that we would have to face the winner that night for the IHSAA State Basketball Championship.

While watching the game, everybody quickly noticed this tall, slim, quick, talented, and deadly left-handed player by the name of Wayne Walls who was destroying his Franklin opponents. I knew that if we were to get by our tough opponent Lafayette Jeff, he and I would most likely square up against each other. In fact, he was so good that I literally went to the locker room halfway through the second quarter (we usually waited until right after half time), as he had inspired me and put a little fear in my heart at the same time. I needed to be sure that I was ready and not distracted. Dressed and ready to go before the rest of the crew entered the locker room, nerves calmed, I got in another quick prayer and had a quick conversation with my angel. I WAS READY!

We would go on to win our twenty-sixth straight game of the year and defeat the third-ranked team in the state, the Lafayette Jeff Broncos, 63–49, to advance to the evening's state championship game. Our mighty Bruins teammates would come up big once again with demonstrating amazing defense, snagging rebounds, shooting timely baskets, retrieving loose balls, and performing their usual winning roles. I would score twenty-six points and grab eight rebounds. Mike Muff dominated the glass, and my back-court mate Tom Madden controlled the tempo of the game from start to finish.

Immediately after the game, our attention turned to the dynamic Wayne Walls and the second-ranked Jeffersonville Red Devils. Knowing that we had a super-quick turnaround for our 8:00 tip-off, we had to eat, get some fluids in our systems, get back to our rooms, and get some rest (for me, sleep). The task was going to be monumental. The

media and college coaches in the region were all familiar
with Jeffersonville, but they didn't have a clue about these
new kids on the block, the Northrop Bruins.

As luck would have it, March Madness was underway,
and one of the best college basketball games I have ever
witnessed was being played when we got back to our rooms.
After playing the entire game earlier and knowing that we
needed to get a nap in, Mike and I just could not stop
watching the mighty UCLA Bruins versus North Carolina
State and David Thompson. The Wolfpack would go on to
upset UCLA, and we saw it as a sign as to what was about
to happen a little later that day. We got a short nap in and
were ready to go!

It was lucky that we did, as little did we know that
Coach Dillie was not going to substitute any of us the
entire game. We were able to escape and yet pull another
upset by topping Wayne Walls and the number-two-ranked
Jeffersonville Red Devils 59–56. Walls would dazzle with 26
points. I would tally 20 points and 7 rebounds, and Mike
Muff would score 10 points and grab 12 huge boards. Once
again, "Big Game" Tom Madden would score 16 points
and dish out 6 assists. "Jumping Jimmy" James Wimbley
would corral 9 big boards and score 7 points (including the
game-clinching free throw). Our six-foot, ten-inch center
Maurice Drinks would give me a much-needed break by
playing superb defense on Wayne Walls for at least half of
the game while also chipping in with three huge baskets.
It was as if my angel were saying, "Congratulations!" as
the loose ball landed in my hands and the horn sounded.
The next day, the headlines would read, "Work of Team
(Teamwork) Difference" and "They Said It Couldn't Be
Done!" We were the champions!

As we stood on the podium to receive our championship rings, my mind quickly drifted to these crazy thoughts

and emotions of the journey, the hard work, and the strong vision. I also reflected on the passing of my mom, her presence and love, and just how grateful I was. After about an hour of on-the-court interviews and wild celebrations, we hopped onto the bus to head back to our rooms at Indiana University's Union Building for a quick team dinner and to greet our families and fans.

While all of this was going on, not one of us had a clue that there had been a major snowstorm happening right in front of us. We would later find out that thousands of fans from all over had to sleep in Assembly Hall that night as all roads were closed due to eight to ten inches of snow. That following morning, we would get up early, pack, eat breakfast, and get on the bus to head home for a huge championship celebration. The local newspaper headlines read: "Bruins Are Champions," "They Said It Couldn't Be Done," and "Work of Team (Teamwork) Different." Upon arrival to the south side of town, we had to board a series of fire trucks, as they would drive north though the city to the Glenbrook Mall where the mayor and literally thousands of our fans would be waiting in the freezing cold to greet, salute, and celebrate with us. One of the loudest applauses came when the mayor called off school for all Fort Wayne public schools on that Monday. As cold as it was, I do not believe that any of us felt a thing. The next morning, the headlines read, "Thousands in Bitter Cold Cheer Champions" and "City Turns Out to Welcome State Basketball Champions." All I could think of was, what a ride, what blessings, what a journey, what a team, what an angel. Thank you, Lord!

Little did I know that I would need that Monday off in the worst way, as I found myself mentally, emotionally, and physically drained. My cup had runneth over! I found some time on that Monday to reflect on what had just happened to me over the previous eight months. Even though I had dreamt this dream, I was not sure that it had just happened for real. I even thought that this real-life deal was even better than the dream.

Even though I had spoken to most of my teammates by phone, and it had been only two days, I could not wait to see them the next day at school. As many of my neighborhood friends and I settled in on the bus, the juke box was blasting, the hugs were warm, the love was real, and laughter could be heard from the bus driver all the way to the back of the bus. It was a bus party going on at 7:30 in the morning!

I am sure that most of us were just as excited about seeing our championship teammates, coaches, cheerleaders, classmates, and fans. Upon arrival, the entire student body would be summoned to the gymnasium as the school would officially reveal our championship trophy, salute our mighty Bruin team, cheerleaders, cheer block, and fans. The local media (print and television), including Mr. Hilliard Gates himself, would be in attendance. Needless to say, no one got anything done that day—or maybe the rest of that school year.

What a dramatic difference from the feeling each of us experienced as we all entered the building on our opening day of school in the September of 1971. Nothing but God! From broken hearts to CHAMPIONS!

This chapter correlates with the real-time, real-life events from the award-winning movie Remember the Titans. The year 1971 was the start of forced nationwide integration, and the movie revealed many of the challenges and incidents that occurred during those times. I remember crying the first time I watched the movie, and many of my classmates claim it as our story. Once again, time after time in our history, the magic of team sports brings communities around the world together.

CHAPTER 11

It's Raining Blessings

ON MONDAY, MARCH 25, 1974, THE school that no one had heard of just three years previously had become the talk of the entire state and region. I had gone from not being on anyone's radar to being named to Indiana's (AP and UPI) First Team All-State, to the Indiana All-Star Team, and a Kentucky Derby All-American. I remember praising God and thinking about all the dreams, the challenges, the sacrifices, the mental and emotional roller coaster rides, the countless hours of sweat, and the grind in the dark when no one was looking. I also remember hearing my mom and Team Jordan (my family) telling me YOU CAN DO IT!

It was now Wednesday, March 27, and I never would have thought that this day would top the unreal and amazing week that I had just experienced. Ten minutes after we settled into our homeroom class, I was summoned to Athletic Director Mark Shoaff's office. Once I arrived, I was informed that a college coach was there waiting to visit with me.

I was speechless to find out that the University of Michigan's head coach, Johnny Orr, was there to see little old me! After our 45-minute meeting, the coach invited me up to Ann Arbor for an official visit to see the school, meet the players, meet with their academic advisors, and spend the weekend on campus. He told me that he wanted to send their private plane to pick me up on Friday. I was shocked, excited, nervous, and scared—I had never been on a plane before!

Knowing I had to keep my composure as the buzz around the school was that Coach Orr was in the building, I headed back to my third-period class. Immediately after lunch, I received notice that I was again needed in Mr. Shoaff's office. I arrived to find that Indiana University's Assistant Coach Bob Donewald was waiting to see me.

To think that at the start of the day that I had a grand total of one official basketball scholarship offer, to NAIA powerhouse Edinburgh State University in Pennsylvania. I still get goose bumps just thinking about those four hours. I was full!

At the end of the day, I was asked to stop by the office as I had some more mail. While a few of my teammates and friends were waiting on me, I crept into the office to retrieve my mail. I was immediately directed to large box sitting on my athletic director's desk with what appeared to be tons of letters (over one hundred)—some were duplicates, but most were handwritten by Division One coaches. My palms were sweating as I quickly stuffed all of them into my book bag. Even though I was super excited to read every word, I had to keep my composure. I also did not want to be boastful or egotistical. I could not wait to get home to open and share all of them with my family.

There were letters from Marquette, Hawaii, North Carolina State, Ball State, Purdue, Michigan State, Minnesota, all my favorites except Norte Dame (my favorite). I had been a huge Irish fan growing up watching

Gary Brokaw, Dwight Clay, and John Shumate upset the might dynasty of UCLA when I was younger. That Friday, I was a nervous wreck as I was shipped off to Ann Arbor in my first-ever plane ride to visit the Michigan Wolverines in their twin-engine airplane. Scared to death, I had a quick talk with my angel (Mom) and prayed.

Toward the end of our senior year, my sidekick partner Mike Muff and I had discussed whether we could play together at the next level. We both were excited about the possibility. Mike was always that fun-loving friend that we all need. Even though neither of us had any interest in attending the University of Hawaii, he suggested that we make that trip on one of our official visits. To think two kids from the same neighborhood, from the same school, even had that opportunity blew us away. We still laugh about that today.

As I tried to navigate through the exciting life-changing series of events without my angel (my mom), I found myself getting off balance, believing the hype, doing things I knew that my mom would not allow or approve of. And even though most of my classmates, teammates, and friends did not know it or would not have believed me, I had discovered girls and start engaging in activities not becoming of what I had been taught, or what I knew was not right until my senior year. Luckily, I soon started dating a young lady who became my high school sweetheart; though she was a cheerleader from our rival school, it seemed to work itself out. Her amazing family would show me a ton of love, give me tons of support, and help get me though a lot of tough times.

Once again, I received some tough love from Team Jordan and my mentor Charles, who had a tougher job than expected of trying to keep me straight, humble, grateful, prayerful, and focused, and of keeping the main things the main things. With three siblings (Willie, Charles, and Lauiretta) attending Indiana University, and the fact that Charles had made the basketball team as a walk-on, favoring IU never became a huge part of our conversations. The strong rumor among most recruiters was that I would be committing to Indiana University.

The one thing I knew right away was that it was especially important to me to stay within a three- to four-hour drive from home, as having my three younger brothers (who were still in school) and the rest of my family close by would mean the world to me. Their support, love, bond, and accountability had become a huge part of my desire to excel. I totally understood the importance of playing for the name on the front of the jersey as well as representing the name on the back of it.

As the letters and offers kept growing, I quickly narrowed my list to Michigan State, Michigan, Marquette, Indiana, and Purdue—and then out of nowhere, I got a phone call from my guy Eugene Parker, who told me that he had to drive down to Purdue (West Lafayette) for an unofficial visit. Of course, out of the mad love and respect I had for him as a person and player, I was honored and decided to go for the ride. He talked about having to decide between Tulane University and Purdue, as he was listed as the number-one recruit for both of those schools. During the drive we discussed our goals, dreams, families, and faith.

Upon arrival, the Purdue coaching staff was shocked that I was there on campus with Eugene, as they had received word that I was a lock to attend IU. They also were expecting to host an all-state player from Illinois by the name of Audie Matthews; he never showed up, as he had just verbally committed to the University of Illinois. Even though an assistant coach mistakenly called me Audie a few times, we had a great visit and an awesome time. During our return trip home, we had real, personal, and deep conversations. We laughed a lot, and we talked about how cool it would be if we ever had a chance to play college ball together.

The following Monday, Purdue put on the full-court press with phone calls, overnight handwritten letters, and a home visit. Most of the schools were recruiting me to player two guard; Purdue also talked about teaming me up in the backcourt with Eugene. The possibilities did get my attention.

Over the next week, Eugene and I saw each other at a couple of local awards banquets. Not long after, he called to inform me that he was going to be a Boilermaker.

After writing down all the pluses and negatives of each school on my list, and after several conversations with my brother Charles and Coach Dillie, I decided that Purdue would be the best fit for me. Eugene and I were elated!

Back at school, it seemed that there were daily celebrations, plenty of laughter, mad love, and just too much fun. Three short years earlier, I could not have dreamt that my senior year would be like this. There was a huge senior prom, tons of city-wide school parties, and extraordinarily little class work getting done. My amazing high school career would be capped off with even more blessings and honors, as I was named the school's Sertoma Award winner (one award for each high school for scholarship, academics, leadership, community service, and sportsmanship). Shortly afterward, I was shocked, deeply humbled, and literally in tears as I was informed that my classmates (80 percent white) had voted for me as their Best Male Citizen Award winner!

A few weeks before graduation, the big news around the state was that my championship rival, future Indiana

All-Star teammate, and in my opinion the best player in the entire Class of 1974, Wayne Walls, had also committed to become a Boilermaker. Honestly, I did not know if I should celebrate or be scared. The only thing I did know for sure was that I had better get back to work.

A month later, Wayne, Larry Bird, and I teamed up to lead our Indiana All-Star team to victories against Russia's national team. We also won our state's two-game annual series against a strong Jack Givens, James Lee (University of Kentucky), and Kenny Higgs (LSU) Kentucky's All-Star team. We had so gained so much respect for each other that we had quickly bonded and become super close friends. We could not wait to officially become Boilermaker teammates.

"Whatever God has for you" (Isaiah 54:17).

CHAPTER 12

Winning and Lessons

THE DAY AFTER WE CELEBRATED OUR high school graduations, Eugene and I were on the phone mapping out our summer workouts and trying to figure out what we needed to have and do for the start of our college careers. We knew that we were going to be roommates and staying in the dorm (Tarkington Hall). We were also told that there were not a lot of social activities offered for the black student body on campus that were not associated with the fraternities, but roller skating was popular. Despite all the noise, we were excited and made up our minds that we were going to have a blast.

Before we knew it, it was move-in day in West Lafayette. I must admit that with no TV or stereo, little clothing, only two pairs of shoes, my toiletries, a winter coat, and my Northrop letter jacket, it did not take my girlfriend and me long to load up the truck of Charles's car and head to Purdue. At first look, we noticed the small room dimensions of 11 feet 7 inches by 16 feet 2 inches, and our beds were just two feet apart. As I said my goodbyes to my girlfriend and brother, it suddenly dawned on me that for the very first time in my life, I would have my own bed. I was excited about that!

As we were settling in on Saturday, we could hear stereos blasting from many rooms in our dorm and on our floor, as everybody had their doors open while moving in. We quickly noticed their massive speakers and stereo equipment; I would later be blown away to find out that many of these freshman classmates had personally build their own stereos. Well, welcome to Purdue, one of the top engineering school in the country!

That night as we walked around campus, there was an unreal upbeat feeling, a crazy festive environment, and mad excitement all around campus. Of course, we made time to stroll over to Mackey Arena, to find the cafeteria and the mailbox, and to meet up with a couple of our new our freshmen teammates, Wayne Walls (Jeffersonville, Indiana) and Mike White (Peoria, Illinois). The four of us got to know each other, formed a bond, and hung out the rest of the day.

On Sunday we hung up a few posters of our favorite players (Doctor J, Kareem, and Pistol) and got our room set up. We also got to meet a few of our dorm neighbors and other athletes who were also housed there. I was thrilled to find out that my guy Fred Arrington (we attended Hanna, Fairfield, Northrop, and now Purdue together), who had earned a full ride to play football for the Boilers, was also a Tarkington resident. We also learned that Fort Wayne natives John Mitchell (track star) and Charles Cammack were assigned to Tarkington as well. Ray Odom (Eugene's cousin and soon to be my good friend) was right next door at Owen Hall. And our new freshman teammates, Wayne Walls and Michael White, were on the other side at Wiley Hall. Everything seemed to be falling in place.

Monday came quickly, as we started our loaded class schedules. We were also to have our first official Boilermaker team meeting and to start our grueling pre-season workouts. My body still hurts thinking about it! Although we had freshman nerves, we were excited about meeting our teammates and the entire coaching staff. We could not wait to get onto the Mackey Arena floor to see how we stacked up against our teammates. We quickly learned that between our class loads, pre-season workouts, and team schedules, the next few months were going to be the toughest of our lives. It did not take long to fall in line, as the coaches monitored everything we did and did not do. The consequences for not being responsible were insane and no fun.

During our home football games, one of the neat things was when our world-class Purdue marching band marched through the campus to head over to Ross-Aide Stadium for the game. Everybody would get excited and would know that it was time to eat lunch and get ready to head over to watch the Boilers. It was during the football season when Wayne, Eugene, Mike White, and I were seated near the Indiana fans at the 50-yard line and it really hit us just how intense, hardcore, nasty, and real the Indiana vs. Purdue rivalry truly was. It was going to be crazy!

It would not be long before our season tip-off banquet. It would be the first time as freshmen that we had a chance to hear what Coach Fred Schaus thought about our progress, development, work ethic, potential, and expectations for the upcoming the season. We had all previously shared our personal thoughts, but we knew that what really mattered was what Coach thought. It carried a lot of weight with us that Head Coach Schaus had been the general manager and head coach of the Los Angeles Lakers with hall of famers Jerry West, Elgin Baylor, and Wilt Chamberlain. It was great to hear that he expected great things from us our first season and our future with the Boilermakers.

By all accounts, this was the prime of some of my all-time favorite artists, athletes, music, and television shows of all time. With the likes of Michael Jackson; Earth, Wind & Fire; Fame; Average White Band; Gladys Knight & the Pips; the Ohio Players; Ali/Frasier; Doctor J, Kareem, Walter Payton; All in the Family; Happy Days; and Sanford and Son, college life was everything we had hoped for and more. On the court, our 1974–75 season was filled with many lessons, challenges, with some measure of success; our Big Ten conference was hands-down ranked as the top conference in America, with the number-one ranked team in the country, Indiana, led by hall of fame coach Bobby Knight, College Player of the Year Scott May, and super-star mates Quinn Buckner, Bobby Wilkerson, and Kent Benson leading the way; and very tough and talented teams Michigan, Minnesota, Michigan State following suit. As freshmen, we quickly learned that it did not matter who the opponent was, winning on the road in the Big Ten was going to be a huge task. Our first collegiate game was against Indiana State, and it did not take us long to find out what all the hype of Mackey Madness was about.

It appeared that Coach Schaus also understood the craziness of it all, as he would insert his four overzealous, athletic, black freshmen with our senior white tough point guard Dick Satterfield into the games together. As soon as we would head to the scorer's table, the Mackey Arena crazies would go nuts; we were quickly dubbed the Soul Patrol. Our coaches, teammates, and everyone watching knew that something good or bad was about to happen.

By game eight, Wayne Walls and I had worked our way into the starting lineup, with Eugene Parker joining us three games later. We would go on to a 17–11 record, finishing third in the Big Ten. One of our major highlights was when Wayne and I were inserted into the starting lineup for our Big Ten opener against a strong Michigan State Spartan team, where we both would score careers highs of 24 (Wayne) and 28 (me) points and lead us to a 93–86 victory. Highlight number two happened on the weekend of my birthday, February 22, with a one-point 83–82 loss to number-one ranked Indiana on national TV, after getting blown out by them a month earlier. We were no longer a secret!

Wayne and Eugene would finish their strong freshman season by averaging 9.6 and 9 points a game, respectively, and being major contributors to our success. I would finish my freshman season second on the team in both scoring (14.1) and rebounding (7.3), and I was selected to a couple of freshman all-American teams. Heading into the season, we understood that only 32 teams would be invited to the NCAA Tournament, with only one certain spot allowed and awarded to the Big Ten. There would be no dancing for the Boilers! Thus, the saying "It's rough in the Big Ten" was repeated by my brother Charles whenever I was faced with a huge challenge for the rest of my life.

The year was full of enjoying pleasant surprises, making adjustments, learning new things, meeting new people, and facing a few challenges. My girlfriend and I also learned that it would be extremely tough and unfair for either of us to maintain a serious relationship with both of our crazy schedules and other challenges. I figured out that I had fallen in love with Purdue and being a Boilermaker. I felt so grateful and blessed for the amazing favor, grace, and opportunity the good Lord had given me. Thinking of my mom, I quickly thought of my season of being one of both winning and lessons.

As the school year was finishing up, I knew that I had to get back home to find a summer job. I didn't know until school started the previous fall that on Sundays the cafeteria was closed and we would be on our own. I had no extra funds to even take a girl to the movies, which was embarrassing. I was able to get a job on the assembly line at Dana Corporation—it was the hardest thing I had ever done up to that point in my life. Working on the line with guys who had been doing those jobs for twenty or thirty years truly taught me life lessons about being a responsible adult, being a man, keeping a work ethic, demonstrating commitment, and doing what real men were willing to do for their loved ones.

All summer long I watched my assembly line co-workers work their butts off and take pride in their work, with zero excuses, while sharing their life stories, lessons, nuggets, and well-wishes for and with me whenever they had a chance! It was truly a humbling experience for a snot-nosed nineteen-year-old kid! Of course, Eugene and I would not allow ourselves to make any excuses for not getting our workouts in (five miles running every day) and practicing our evening hoops at the Old Fort YMCA, where all the great Fort Wayne ballers hooped. Little did I know that would be my routine for two out of my next three summers.

In June, shortly after arriving home, my girlfriend and I found out that we were going to be parents. This quickly put my life and everything in it into a clear sense of urgency. The tough-love conversations we had with her parents and my older siblings were among the hardest I ever had at that point in my life. Through it all, at no time did she or her awesome parents speak about getting an abortion, putting pressure on me, or forcing me to quit school. It was all about love, support, confidence, and their belief in me to do the right things moving forward. One thing I knew for sure was that my child was going to be extremely blessed to have her as a mom and her amazing parents as his grandparents. My brilliant, handsome, healthy, and remarkable son, Jamarcus, would be born six months later. Thank you, Lord!

There was also now a tremendous buzz surrounding the upcoming Boiler season, as superstar and Indiana's Mr. Basketball, Kyle Macy, had committed to attending Purdue. Boiler Nation was jacked! Only two games into our season, we would lose tough, seasoned, gifted, senior leader and point guard Bruce Parkinson to injury for the entire year. With Macy and freshman Jerry Sichting, we felt confident that we would be okay. The Boilers' schedule would once again be one of the toughest in the country, with road trips to California against the legendary Coach Jonnie Wooden and the mighty UCLA Bruins (bookends All-Americans Richard Washington and Marcus Johnson), West Virginia, and to Butler; and home games versus Providence, Xavier, and the University of California before the stacked Big Ten schedule. We would once again finish third in the Big Ten, with Indiana and Michigan advancing to the Big Dance. Four of our opponents that year would end up reaching the Final Four (Rutgers, Michigan, UCLA, and Indiana). It's rough in the Big Ten!

I would finish the season leading the team in both scoring (17 ppg) and rebounding (9.2). My classmate and roommate Eugene tallied 15 ppg, and our defensive star and partner Wayne Walls chipped in 11 ppg and 7 boards every night. Macy would prove to be a joy to play with, as he finished his superb freshman season scoring at a 14-points-per-game clip, with a few big-time games along the way. As the school year wound down, it was hard to believe that we were about to enter our junior year in college. Oh well, back to the Fort (hometown) to get to work on my summer assembly-line job. Even though it was the hardest physical labor I ever had to do, those summers were priceless, as my co-workers taught me so much about real life, accountability, hard work, positivity, commitment, and true love.

Over the remainder of the summer, my trusted and treasured brother Eugene and I would chat about life challenges, decisions we made, our expectations as leaders, and our insane and tough upcoming 1976–77 basketball schedule. We would open with road games against nationally ranked Alabama, Miami (OH), and Providence. Indiana State (Larry Bird), Louisville (Darryl Griffin), Arizona, Georgetown, Butler, and Manhattan rounded out our crazy non-conference schedule. Big Ten rivals Indiana (Mike Woodson, Kent Benson, and company); Minnesota (Mychal Thompson and Ray Williams); Michigan (Rickey Green and Phil Hubbard); Northwestern (Billy McKinney); Wisconsin (Wes Matthews); Michigan State (Greg Kessler) all looked to fight for one (or two) of the thirty-two spots that were going to be heading to the NCAA tournament. One thing I loved about our team was that we all took pride and we loved playing in the big games in the brightest lights.

Halfway through the summer, we got the sad news that Kyle Macy was going to transfer to the University of Kentucky. But a few weeks later, we received a commitment from a seven-foot big man from Denver by the name of Joe Berry Carroll. The must-needed summer grind was now in full effect, as our Boiler crew had all decided that we were all in. And that it was our time to go dancing!

The national buzz about our now seasoned team was everywhere, as we arrived on campus a few days earlier than normal. We wanted to make sure that we were prepared for our class schedules and were ready to get to work. We loved to go over to the Co-Rec building (for all things student sports) to play some hoops with football players and other students. It was a great time of bonding, fun, and competition as many of the football players were also talented high school basketball players.

It was days before our first Boiler football game when we had gotten word in the Purdue Exponent (our daily student newspaper) that one of my favorite guys, Fred Arrington, was making all kinds of noise on the gridiron and was projected to be a starting linebacker for the Boilers. I could not wait to see him play. Fred would go on to be named an all-Big Ten performer and would become the very first ever defensive player in Purdue's history to earned Most Valuable Player honors for his team.

I love football, and I absolutely loved walking over to Ross-Aide with our fans and my teammates to watch our gridiron brothers play. We all were like family. We loved each other and were emotionally attached at the hip. Imagine a college campus full of its football and basketball stars learning the power of edification by walking around campus loudly yelling at each other, "You're great!" or "You're the greatest!" And it did not matter if we were with our girls or who was around. Little did we know that something that we thought was so small and silly would create a winning, loving, and positive environment. It was amazing to watch how quickly our circle grew and the impact it had on our entire campus. With that overflow of support and the genuine love from our peeps, we were given even more juice to represent our school. We could've waited to get prime seats to root for each other. Here is the kicker: Today, forty-five years later, we still privately remind each other of our greatness. On top of that, when any of us has had personal life or health challenges, we always show up.

There should have been a law against the amount of fun we had in West Lafayette during those years. I will be eternally grateful for my Boiler Dawgs, the love, and the memories—we are brothers for life. RIP to my brothers Eugene Parker and Ronnie Moore, who personified greatness. Thank you, Lord!

After opening our season with a couple of humbling tough road losses at nationally ranked Alabama and at Miami, it did not take us long to come back down to earth and realize that we were going to get everybody's best shot. We would rebound and go on to win fourteen of our next sixteen games. We would defeat Indiana twice on our way to finishing second in the Big Ten with a 20–8 record. We were one of only thirty-two teams that would be heading to the Big Dance!

The draw called for us to pair up against Hall of Fame Coach Dean Smith, all-American Phil Ford, and the powerful North Carolina Tarheels. Just to make it a little bit tougher, we would have to beat them on their home floor, as they were the regional tournament host. After a back-and-forth dog fight the entire game, we were able to take a six-point lead with three minutes to go, only to turn the ball over several times, get behind, and let them get into Phil Ford's masterful three-corners time. Our season ended with a 69–66 defeat at the hands of North Carolina.

I would have my best season as a Boilermaker, as I scored at an 18.6 per game clip and was named the team's MVP. I was on the AP/UPI and coaches' first team All-Big Team, and I was invited to join thirty-plus of the best college players in the country to try out for the USA World University Games. These would be led by the University of Louisville's legendary coach Denny Crum, whom we had played against twice in my collegiate career. Even though I was emotionally, physically, and mentally exhausted, I was excited about the huge opportunity to represent our country and play with some of the best players in the game.

At that time I had fallen in love with my college sweetheart, and for the first time ever, I was planning to take a couple of weeks off just to relax with her as we headed into our senior year.

After tryouts, this skinny, piss-poor kid from the heart of the inner city in Fort Wayne, Indiana, was summoned back to the University of Louisville's campus as I learned that I would be teaming up with such big-time college stars as the University of Arkansas' Sidney Moncrief, Louisville's Darry Griffin, Michigan's Phil Hubbard, Indiana State's Larry Bird, Portland State's Freeman Williams, and several others to prepare for our trip to Sofia, Bulgaria. We would represent the USA in an attempt to bring home the gold medal for our country. The two-per-day workouts and scrimmages were intense, and they were mentally and physically tough, as everyone was battling for both respect and playing time.

I have crazy memories of that tournament, especially of tempers flaring in our USA–Cuba matchup. We were tied 46–46 with 18 minutes remaining in the game. The benches were emptied, and fights broke out in front of the U.S. bench. Bulgarian police stepped in and regained order, and when the game resumed, we stormed out to a 94–78 victory. Calvin Natt led the U.S. with 24 points and Griffith added 21, with Williams scoring 19 points and Griffith adding 15. Afterwards, we defeated Brazil 103–81. Before downing Czechoslovakia 85–69, we earned the right to play in the championship game, with Calvin Natt and me leading the way with 19 points each. We would go on to finish 8–0 and blow out the favorite, the mighty Soviet Union team, in the gold medal game.

After we arrived back in the States, I realized that I was only a few days away from the start of my senior year of college. This also meant that I was close to starting our team's pre-season workouts. Once I returned to campus, I had a scheduled meeting with Coach Schaus, as he wanted to check on me. He informed me that I could take a week off if I needed to. As a leader, senior, and captain, I strongly felt that not participating with my teammates was not an option. My body said I need to do it, but my heart and mind told me that I needed to be there.

I had already felt bad as we had five new freshmen join our crew that I did not know and had not spent any time with. Between keeping up with my loaded class schedule, participating in preseason workouts, bonding with my new teammates, hanging out with my friends, learning to play with a much improved and future great big man for the first time, and searching for some quality time to spend with my girlfriend, it was going to be tough. For some reason, as our official practices began, Eugene, Wayne, and I would talk about something being a little out of sync; we did not know what it was, but we knew that we needed to get it figured out before the start of our senior year.

We started the season ranked number 12 in the country, defeating Xavier, and then dropped to number 17 after a blow-out upset road loss to crazy, fired-up Indiana State and the USA and Indiana All-Star teammate Larry Bird. He had warmed me all summer that they were going to get us when we came to Terre Haute, Indiana. It was their game of the year, and the fans and players all behaved like it. We seemed to be back on track after defeating Alabama, Arizona State, and Arizona on the road. The success would be hit and miss the entire year, as we would split battles with Indiana, defeat Minnesota with former NBA All-Stars Kevin McHale and Mychal Thompson, defeat Michigan twice, upset Magic Johnson and the Michigan State Spartans (my best game as a Boiler—28 points and 12 rebounds), and get upset by both Northwestern and

Illinois, to end my college career 16–7 and fourth in the Big Ten.

After the game, we all found out in the media that Coach Fred Schaus announced that he was retiring, effective immediately. I was devastated. Along with us seniors not holding up our end of the bargain, I had always wondered if his unannounced retirement plans were part of the out-of-sync feeling we were experiencing all year. I was sad, as I would have liked to think that we might have been able to use it to rally the troops.

As a leader, after every defeat, I would ask myself what I could have done better to help us win. Even though I would once again be named the team's MVP and to the AP, UPI, and the coaches' first team all-Big Ten teams, I felt that I could have done more and been better. It was a hard pill to swallow that my college career was over, and we would not be going dancing. I knew that the real world was waiting, and I was not quite sure if I was ready for it.

After my long summer representing the USA, the preseason conditioning, a tough year of classes, and our insane basketball schedule, I found myself emotionally, mentally, and physically drained, and I needed a break in the worst way. With receiving a couple of invitations to all-star college games, selecting an agent, anticipating the fast-approaching NBA draft, working with Purdue's basketball camp, and helping my fiancée plan our June wedding, it did not take long for me realize that the break wasn't coming anytime soon. God was at work, and I needed to be on the move.

CHAPTER 13

Ouch!

ALL SUMMER, MY AGENT KEPT ME informed on my draft potential and possibilities. Many of the agents, basketball publications, and NBA experts had me listed as one of the top six small forwards in the country. They projected I would be chosen at the end of the first round or as a middle of the second-round draft pick.

In 1976, the famed ABA (American Basketball Association) ceased its operations and took hundreds of jobs off the table. For financial reasons, the NBA cut their rosters from twelve to eleven, so there were now only 242 NBA jobs available. And on top of all of that, the New Jersey Nets were engaged in a lawsuit as they were attempting to move from the Nassau Coliseum to New Jersey, a move the Knicks said could not be made without their approval.

On draft day, I was working the Purdue Basketball Camp. My agent was in New York keeping in touch with me via the Purdue basketball office with updates. The first call came early in the day, when he said that it appeared I would go at the end of the first round to the Los Angeles Lakers. Several hours later, in what seemed like a full day, he finally called to inform me that word had gotten out among the teams that I had a bad knee. He asked me if I ever had a problem with anybody at Purdue, and I told him that I was not aware of any. I had grown three inches during my college career. I had never missed a game or practice, but I had a slight case of tendonitis (growing pains). I had fallen to the fourth-round pick of those New Jersey Nets, with no chance of a guaranteed contract. The odds of fulfilling my mama's dream of becoming a pro seemed slim.

Unexpectedly, the following week, in the middle of attending summer school, I was summoned and given five days to fly to New Jersey for their rookie/free-agent camp. Once there, we were informed that only five of us (out of twenty-plus) would be invited back to the veterans' camp. After the toughest two-a-day practices I had ever experienced, I was invited back. My body had never endured such pain.

I would sign a non-guaranteed contract. I played the entire pre-season schedule, and I would earn a spot in the nine-man rotation. I scored in double digits in a few games, and I was told to start searching for an apartment with the Nets number-one draft choice Winford Boynes, who I prayed would become my new friend and teammate. The final day of camp, I was informed by Coach Kevin Loughery that "they tried to find a way to keep me, but they couldn't afford to keep me." They also cut one of their long-time veterans who had a guaranteed contract. It was disappointing in that it was the last day of camp when everybody was finalizing rosters and there was no time to give me a shot. For the first time in my life, I did not like the business of basketball. I felt as if I had let my mom and my family down.

A week later, I received a call that I was selected first round with a brand-new league called the Western

Basketball Association (WBA), with teams in great cities on the West Coast: Las Vegas, Tucson, Reno, Fresno, Salt Lake, Tri-Cities, and Great Falls. The coaches were all well-known and of high quality, including Herb Brown, Bill Musselman, and John Wetzel, just to name a few. The salaries were far better than other options that were on the table. I would live in the Tri-Cities (Kennewick, Pasco, and West Richland) and play for the Washington Lumberjacks, and I would earn first team all-league honors. We would finish with the second-best record in the league and lose to the eventual league champions. After our playoff loss, our team had decided to pack up and go out on the town together prior to all of us traveling back to our hometowns the following day. We had a blast, as I really enjoyed the season, coaches, city, amazing competition, and my teammates.

It was in reality an early night for my wife and me, as we knew that we still had to check out of our apartment, load up the car, and drive home to Indy. As I got up in the middle of the night, I collapsed. I knew I was not drunk or high (I did not get high)—I just had my limit of one beer. My wife Kathy thought that I was joking as she turned on the lights, and we saw that both of my knees and ankles had swollen to twice their size.

I remember immediately going into prayer, as I was in complete panic mode. As fate would have it, the following morning my agent would call to inform me that the Denver Nuggets were down a man and were looking to sign me for the upcoming playoffs and the last few games of their regular season. In tears, I could not even mention my current situation. I think I prayed all day and iced my entire body, hoping and praying that whatever it was would just disappear. This was just not right! He would call me back to get information for them to fly me out, at which time I had to finally tell him the truth. I am tearing up now just thinking about it.

I make matters even worse; Kathy would have to do the heavy lifting and drive the long 2,100 miles home to Indianapolis herself. I was in pain, I was having a pity party, and I could not walk. Upon arriving at home, we quickly set up appointments with several medical professionals. The third doctor finally found the proper diagnosis—I had a rare infection called Reiter's Syndrome, which affects only 20,000 people worldwide every year. Joint pain and swelling were triggered by some form of an infection in my body. I was experiencing joint pain and stiffness, mostly in the knees, ankles, and feet. The prognosis was that there was no treatment, but I would have to stay off my feet (not a problem) and pray. I was told that recovery could take anywhere from two to six months—or it could affect me for the rest of my life.

Suddenly, the main thing in my life was no longer dreaming of playing in the NBA, but just to be able to walk, to not be a burden on anybody, and to just live a healthy life. As a man, not being able to help contribute to my household and wife was hurting my soul. I was basically an infant, as I literally had to have someone cook for me and bring me meals. I also would have to crawl back and forth to the restroom. As cocky and prideful as I was, this one was going to be tough.

With Kathy having to work a full-time job and take care of our household needs, I called my awesome big sister Suzette (in Fort Wayne, Indiana) to ask her to take me in. Even though she had three beautiful girls and a husband, there was no hesitation. It was the best situation possible, as I slept on a mat on their basement floor, with the bathroom a few feet away. I also had television and much-needed personal privacy. My big sister, my awesome brother-in-law Richard, and their brilliant and gorgeous daughters (Shonda, Richelle, and Nana) treated me with tons of love and respect and lifted my spirits in ways they would never know.

In the middle of this storm, I was reminded of something my mom would say, that there would be times in your life when you will not only have to drop to your knees, but crawl. In real time, I could honestly say that I got it. Five months later, the good Lord would heal my body, renew my spirits, refresh my mind, and enable me to be more determined and focused than ever.

My trust in God and my faith led me to believe that I was going to be better, stronger, and wiser than ever before. After six months, the good Lord blessed me to complete recovery. It did not take long after that to get back into my new routine of eating everything in sight, running five miles every day, honing light individual skills and shooting drills, and lifting light weights. I would also head over to the Old Fort Y to battle the awesome talent in the city during the week, and I would travel all over the city with my brothers and friends to find or create competitive games on the weekends. Most of the players had no clue what I had just gone through. I kept hearing a lesson learned: ***It is better to be prepared for an opportunity and not get one, than getting one and not being prepared.*** I had made up my mind that I was going to be ready. Now I needed just one more opportunity.

CHAPTER 14

Perseverance!

NOW STAYING AT MY FATHER'S HOUSE, I had just completed my morning workout on a hot July day when the phone rang. I was exhausted and did not feel like answering.

"Hi, Walter Jordan?" a voice asked.

"Yes, sir, this is he."

"Walter, this is Coach Bill Musselman from University of Minnesota."

"Hi, Coach!"

"Walter, the reason I am calling you is to let you know that I have watched you play while you were in high school. I tried to recruit you and coached against you the four years you were at Purdue, and I want to let you know that tomorrow I will be named the head coach of the Cleveland Cavaliers."

I was completely silent!

Coach continued, "Anyway, I believe that you belong in the NBA, and I want to personally invite you to come and play for the Cavs in our Los Angles NBA Summer League team."

"What! When?" I sputtered. "Yes, sir, Coach Musselman! When do you need me there?"

"We get started in a couple of weeks. I will have my secretary give you a call later this week to book your flight and your itinerary."

I was jacked! There was a huge pep in my step and I did not sleep that night.

Upon arrival and check in, we were immediately given our physicals and got to meet with our new teammates and coaches. I was pleasantly surprised when I saw a few players I had watched or heard about, Bill Laimbeer and Bruce Flowers of Notre Dame, and the former Houston Rockets first-round pick six-foot, eleven-inch Lee Johnson. That evening we started our very tough, physical, and intense preparations. It appeared that we all (including the coaches) had chips on our shoulders and were deeply engaged.

At one of our earlier games, during team warm up, I kept hearing an awfully familiar voice shouting out such things as "Old Fort Y, the fire station, McCulloch Center, the Reservoir"—different hooping locations from my childhood. When I finally located the voice, it was my guy, my best childhood friend, my brother Ray Causey. I was blown away! I knew he had moved to Los Angeles and thought about him often, but just as he had always done, he just showed up. It was so special as he, along with my partner Mike Muff, had been a big part of my long hard journey and my dream of playing in the NBA. To say that I had some extra juice was an understatement.

Our summer league team would go on to advance to the championship game against NBA star Bernard King (who was fighting back from a team alcohol suspension) and the Golden State Warriors team, which was being broadcast by a new station called ESPN. It was a huge opportunity and a challenge for me personally, as I had tremendous respect and love for Bernard. As I competed against and was briefly teammates with the Nets, he always gave me encouragement and respect. He made sure to come by to tell me, "Don't quit; you belong in this league" when I was the last player released a day before the regular season began.

I also admired Bernard for his professionalism, work ethic, passion, and love for the game. Knowing that the entire league would be watching our loaded talent of free agents, and my personal match up with Bernard, I had to get in a few extra prayers and plenty of rest the night before. Bernard would be his usual unstoppable and super self, so I knew that I had to compete, not back down, be aggressive, and play as hard as I possible against him. Lee Johnson, Bill Laimbeer, and I (25 points and 8 rebounds) would all play well, and we would win the LA Summer League Championship. In the days following, we would all be offered guaranteed contracts by several NBA teams. I received offers from both the Houston Rockets and the Cleveland Cavaliers. The decision was made easy by Coach Musselman's loyalty and his confidence in me. He told me that he loved my work ethic and attitude, and he had been indirectly engaged in my career over the previous six years. It was also exciting to find out that my summer league teammate, Bill Laimbeer, had also decided to join us in Cleveland.

The Cavs arena was in Richfield, Ohio, not downtown Cleveland, so it was closer if we lived in Akron, Ohio. At the start of training camp, I quickly realized that it was going to be a war, as the most talented and challenging roster spot fights were going to be at my position. There was the team's leading scorer Mike Mitchell, and seasoned veterans Kenny Carr, Richard Washington, and Don Ford. The two-a-day practices were the toughest, most physical, and most challenging sessions I had ever experienced, just

as Coach Musselman had warned us that they would be.
A quick bite to eat, a hot bath or shower, and a quick nap
were required between and after each practice; many times,
I found myself asking if my body was going to hold up. I
kept hearing my dad's voice: "No excuses"; and my brother's voices: "Stop crying, you big sissy"; and "Suck it up—
you're tougher than that. Get it done!"

Once the season began, I found myself building great
relationships with our two best players and our captains,
Mike Mitchell and Randy Smith. For some reason, they
took me under their wings and would invite me to tag
along with them on our road trips. Whenever we hung out
after our home games, I was at a good place mentally and
emotionally.

Early in the year, we were playing the Supersonics in
Seattle, and Mike was having a terrible shooting game.
During timeouts and in the middle of the game, many of
us could hear him asking the coach to put me in the game
to replace him, but for whatever reason, Coach never did.
It was thought that he was sending a message to everybody
that he was the coach, and no one was going to tell him
how to do his job. Mike and everybody else could see that
he simply was not having his best day. I was personally
disappointed, as I thought that Coach Musselman has the
utmost respect for and confidence in my abilities. I was not
so sure anymore.

The other assistant coaches would always tell me to
be patient as my time would be coming soon. For some
reason, it always appeared that I would get more playing
time on the road and when our owner was not in attendance. Several days later, we were playing the Los Angeles
Lakers at the Forum, and Coach Musselman told me to be
ready as I was going to get my chance that night. I was fired
up as I would be going up against my idol Kareem Abul

Jabbar, Jamaal Wilkes, my college rival Magic Johnson, and my favorite team, the Lakers.

I would not enter the game until the beginning of the fourth quarter when we were down sixteen points. I played well and would go on to score eight out of the team's next twelve points to pull us within eight, before losing by eight. Late in the game, I would twist my right ankle after landing on Kareem's foot going after a rebound—not smart against his seven feet three inches! But there was no way I was going to let the trainer or the coach know that I was in pain until after the game. While icing my ankle in the locker room after the game, all the players and the coaches were commenting on how well I had played. Coach Musselman told the team that I would be starting the next night in Portland if I was physically ready to go.

Leaving the Forum on crutches, and with my past injury history, I was fearful of another setback. Instead of having another pity party, I knew that I needed to reach out to my angel and my God. No sleep for me, as I was told to ice it all night and summon the trainer the first thing in the morning. When he arrived, he noticed that the swelling had gone down, but there appeared to be a fracture, so he drove me to get a quick MRI. The results were positive, and I was projected to be done for at least four to six months. Not good! My teammates, our coaches, and finally our owner were confident and excited about my becoming part of our eight-man rotation. I could not wait to get healthy enough to start my rehab, as I was more confident than ever that I could perform at the NBA level.

The following year, I fractured my other foot early in pre-season and would be placed on injured reserve. At this time, I was contemplating going overseas to play, as it did not appear that my body could to endure the NBA daily grind of two-a-day practices and an eight-month season.

When I factored in the tax-free salary, free rent, leased car, once-a-day practices, one game a week, a new culture, and being the star player, it was a no-brainer. Badalona, Spain, here I come! It would be some of the most enjoyable times I ever had playing basketball. My teammates, the owners, and fans from the entire country were amazing. After being named one of the best foreign players in the country, the next season, one of the best organizations and teams in Spain, Juventud, came calling. Life was good!

After two years in Spain, several NBA teams reached out to invite me to their free agent camps. My agent felt that it would be a great idea to at least use them as a negotiation bluff to my European suitors. Of course, I would be interested in being closer to home, so I was willing to listen. All players invited to NBA camps had to sign a contract prior to attending any free agent camp. As a serious bluff, I signed with the Kansas City Kings camp. I then opted out after a few days after getting word from my agent that I had several teams preparing to make me great offers. I needed to be ready to leave in a few days.

All set and ready to fly out of the country, my agent received a call from Ron Behagen, a former NBA player, that I would no longer be able to play professionally in Europe, as there was a recent law on the books that did not allow NBA players who played in Europe, and then signed or played another NBA contract, to ever return to play in Europe. What in the hell just happened?

By that time, NBA teams were finalizing their rosters, and it was too late to try to revisit any of the former camp offers I missed out on. I was trying to figure out my next move, as I knew that I had to keep playing, stay in shape, and let everyone know that I was still here. The season had started, so my options were extremely limited at that point. After all that I had been through, I was not overly excited about playing, traveling sometimes nine to eleven hours in a van with nine or ten extra-long men, or in challenging winter weather on the East Coast. Enter the Continental Basketball Association (CBA), the longtime home and best minor league for the NBA.

I was informed that the Detroit Spirits of the CBA somehow had my rights, so as I mentally prepared to head out to the Motown city, I was informed that my former NBA coach Gerald Oliver (Cavs assistant) was now the head coach and general manager of the Toronto Tornadoes (first ever professional basketball team in Canada) and had just traded for my rights. Now I was excited, as I had a great relationship and a ton of respect for Coach Oliver.

It did not take me long to adjust and fall in love with the breathtaking city of Toronto, my teammates, and our diehard fans. I was delighted to find out that the talent and the league were going to extremely tough and challenging. It included many past and future NBA players, with future NBA Hall of Fame coaches Phil Jackson, George Karl, Bill Musselman, and others. My teammates included Robert Smith (UNLV), Lewis Jackson (Alabama State), Greg Hines (Hampton), Peter Thibeaux (St. Mary's College), Ron Crevier (Boston College), Paul Brozavich (UNLV), Wayne Abrams, (SIU), Derrick Pope (Ohio State), Ralph Jackson (UCLA), and Reggie Gaines. We were very close, as we were all housed in the Holiday Inn in downtown Toronto for the season. We spent a crazy amount of time together and knew that every night we would have to bring our hard hats and lunch buckets. No nights off!

Once I arrived, Coach O (Oliver) made several additional trades, as we fell behind in the standings in our attempt to make the playoffs; the year before (their first), we did not get there. After several team meetings, we made a commitment to go down fighting. We would go on to win eight out of ten, defeat the league's three top teams, and put ourselves right in the middle of the playoff picture. For financial reasons, with about a month to go, Coach O was fired. Our owner, former Cleveland Cavs owner and now my good friend Ted Stepien, whose keen vision was to bring an NBA franchise to Canada, had asked me if I would consider being the team's player/head coach. I was completely caught off guard!

After much prayer and a few phone calls, I declined the generous, humbling, and mind-blowing offer. As one of the team's leaders and a co-captain, I felt a special and unique connection with my teammates and didn't want to hinder or take a chance of losing the great bond, brotherhood, and momentum we had heading into the playoffs. With our back against the wall, we would go on a 15–2 run at the end of the season to earn final playoff spot in the Eastern Division.

A few weeks later, we would lose a hard-fought nail-biter series 3–2 to the defending Eastern Division champs Albany Patroons, coached by future NBA Hall of Famer Coach Phil Jackson. To this day, I am always teased about how much Coach Jackson's life and my life would have been completely different had I taken the job and we had won that series.

The next year, our Toronto franchise had to move, and I was still being invited to NBA training camps. By now, I was very experienced and knowledgeable about how the professional basketball game was being played, and I did not like it. I was listed as a quality player, with high character, who anyone could bring into training camp with no drama, who could be signed with a small signing bonus and a decent non-guaranteed contract. Let them battle to get the veterans and guaranteed contract players ready for the season, with a very slim chance of making the team.

Over the next several years, I would go on to play for teams in Italy and Hawaii (one year); and partial years in Utica, New York; Great Falls, Montana (for future NBA Coach George Karl); and Albany, New York (Coach Phil Jackson). A long time before, I had decided that I was not going to play anymore after I reached thirty years of age. In my last go around, one of Coach Jackson's best front-line players got injured several weeks before the playoffs, and he asked me to join his Albany Patroons team. Out of respect for Coach, I did.

Though it was a shortened season, it was one of the most rewarding experiences I ever had playing basketball, but it was not the stuff on the floor but the stuff off of it that truly impacted my life. Coach Jackson and his long-time friend, author and coach Charlie Rosen, introduced us to the power of practicing meditation, reading good books, exercising personal self-discipline, and having a strong vision and a belief system. I would also bond and connect with teammate Kenny Natt (NBA player and long-time coach) to become lifetime friends and brothers.

I was excited about making this one last run as we were projected to go far in the playoffs and were the favorite to win it all. But as fate would have it, an old friend named Injury decided to show its ugly face once again. I would twist my knee days before our second round and would be done for the season. It was a tough way to go out, but I was extremely grateful that the good Lord granted me all those years to fulfill my mom's last words, to see the world, get a great education, collect amazing memories, have tons of laughs, build incredible relationships, experience insane growth, and to play this sometimes unforgiving and phenomenal game that I fell in love with when I was twelve years old.

CHAPTER 15

Community Servant

HEADING TO THAT NEXT CHAPTER OF my life, I discovered that I was starting to get excited about whatever it was that the good God had planned for me. For the first time in two decades, I knew that I no longer had to take my body through those tough grinds and extreme challenges. What I did know was that I loved my community and wanted to get back home to Fort Wayne, Indiana, and give back some of the support that was granted to me. The respect, prayers, and unconditional love were impossible to ever ignore or forget.

In the progress of trying to figure out my next move, I placed a call to a great friend and told him that I was considering moving back home. I was looking for a quality job until I figured out my next move. Twenty minutes later, I received a phone call from a well-respected friend and successful business owner, asking me to consider coming to work for him. Just like that, it was done. Ain't God good!

On May 9, 1980, during the summer months, I was blessed to call on many of my relationships to help fulfill the promise I had made to my wonderful middle school citizenship class teacher, Miss Betty Stein; my special little girlfriend, Kimberly; and myself. The Walter Jordan's Parade of Stars benefit basketball game was formed, which would assist the Allen County Society for Crippled Children and Adults and the Big Brothers Big Sisters.

The annual event would tip off with many of Fort Wayne's former city and local stars at Northrop High School and would grow larger than my wildest dreams. These stars included Mike Muff (Murray State), Eugene Parker, Mr. Basketball Jim Master (Kentucky), Tim Smiley (Edinboro State), Alonzo Craig (Edinboro State), and others.

Three years later, the game had moved to a standing-room-only crowd at IPFW. An overflow crowd included fans stacked under the baskets at both ends, and hundreds of fans were turned away. We were blessed to recruit former IU stars Mike Woodson and Butch Carter and national champs Isiah Thomas and Ray Tolbert. Houston Rockets star Robert Reid also showed up for our cause.

In 1986, NBA all-star and slam-dunk champion Dominique Wilkins scored 51 points and NBA all-star Ron Harper scored 49 as the East beat the West 184–180 for another sellout IPFW crowd. The two also battled Fort Wayne's John Flowers (UNLV) in the slam-dunk contest before Wilkins won.

The following year was magical, remarkable, nerve-wracking, and special even before our game. I was in the hospital with my wife during her thirty-plus hours of labor, and my beautiful, precious daughter Asha was born. Having to fit this long body into a hospital chair over-night, sleepless, exhausted, sore, and stressed; trying to stay connected and in contact with our star players, volunteers, the media, welcoming committee, officials, and others; it was well worth it all. My beautiful daughter's birth seemed to give me renewed strength, energy, and motivation. She had stolen the show even before it began!

A couple of days later, Dominique Wilkins and Ron Harper returned for a rematch in the dunk contest. The game had been moved once again to the Memorial Coliseum to accommodate our crowd of well over 8,000 excited fans. There were 49 dunks in the game with an all-star game quality roster. The stars included Wayman Tisdale (RIP, my friend), Chuck Person, Adrian Dantley, Johnny Dawkins, Spud Webb, and Scott Skiles.

As exciting as the games were, the players and community also seemed to enjoy our annual after-game dinner parties. They were hosted every year by our community hero, millionaire businessman, mentor, and late great friend Mr. Link Chapman. The players loved the first-class soul-food feast, the festive party, the welcoming environment, and the love and respect awarded to them.

After ten years, because Larry Bird, Magic, and other NBA stars formed their own summer all-star games, the NBA pulled its sanction of our game, threatening to fine players who participated. Such NBA and college stars as Ron Harper; Illinois's Kenny Battle and Ken Norman; Indiana's Jay Edwards and Ray Tolbert; NBA stars Shawn Kemp and Scooter and Rodney McCraw; Purdue's Doug Lee and Everette Stephens; and UAB star Tracy Foster would help us go out with a bang. The halftime slam-dunk contest was amazing as Tolbert, Harper, Battle, Kemp, Stevens, and Mitchell competed. Harper, Kemp, and Battle advanced to the finals where Battle won it with a 360-degree tomahawk. Thousands of dollars were raised for our community, forever friendships were formed, and a lifetime of memories was granted.

Once again, I was in awe of God's grace and what happens when God grants you favor. Early on, many of my loyal, committed, and awesome friends would simply tell me, "Let me know the date, what you need me to do, and I'll be there!" These included the late great Mr. Tom Knox (former ABA official), NBA official Danny Crawford, official Ronnie Knox, Vernon "Punkin" Allison (25 years of partnership and commitment to me and my programs— RIP, brother), Robert Ridley (Parade of Stars assistant for 10 years), Anthony Beasley, Willie Jordan (uniforms and programs designer), and the late great Mr. Hilliard Gates. My brother Eugene Parker (RIP), Coach Gene Keady, Larry Tinker, Raymond Odom, the amazing Indiana Pacers Pacemates, our entire sportscasters and media, and a bus load of amazing community volunteers, entertainers, donors, and my entire family were also on board. None of this happened without each of them. I am so grateful for them believing, encouraging, praying for, loving, and sharing my vision.

Still with plenty of community and youth initiatives on my bucket list, I would start an intimate group of young black professionals and close friends to form "JustUs," which was designed to contribute to the immediate needs and issues that were affecting our youth, families, and community. Seeing that our basketball-crazy city did not offer a quality summer hoops program for our youth, I started the Walter Jordan's Future Stars Summer Basketball League, which was held twice a week at our downtown YWCA. Our goal was to provide a safe, positive environment where upcoming young talent could develop, be surrounded with positive mentors, and grow. Boys and girls would be assigned to teams and would play twice a week in the evenings (including playoffs) in a controlled and structured setting.

For ten years, it became the summer hoop home where all the city's future stars in elementary, middle, and high school came to compete, show off their skills, and improve. Most of the teams were coached by former high school players and successful community leaders. It has been an absolute blessing and so rewarding to follow their growth, development, missteps, accomplishments, and lives over the years. Thank you, Lord!

Being a serious music lover, and having lived in lived in different countries, I had grown accustomed to having high-level entertainment options and opportunities, which I as a kid I knew were extremely limited in my hometown. So I started Jordan Promotions, LLC, where many of the top R&B and jazz artists (Keith Sweat, Roy Ayers, Melissa Morgan, Loose Ends, Herbie Hancock, Al B Sure, Najee, Johnny Kemp, Tony-Tonie-Tone', Kenny G, and others) would come into town to perform for us. The support was outstanding, and it was tons of fun. The only challenge was not out-pricing ourselves based on our small ventures and market size. The high risk of fifty percent of the funds having to be paid out at the signing of the agreement, without a ticket being sold (in a last-minute purchasing town), did not make things easier. This was another thing off my bucket list. The relationships built during these five years were worth a million bucks!

Loving people as I do, I accepted a fun spare-time job representing and working as a regional spokesperson for the Indiana Hoosier Lottery. I would record a weekly lottery question, "Ask Walter Jordan," with the winners awarded lottery tickets and prices. I would also attend many Hoosier Lottery-sponsored community events. The most rewarding parts of the job were educating individuals about the lottery, meeting some incredible statewide leaders and other people, and witnessing the good that a lot of the money can do for our communities. The tough part was seeing them not investing in their minds or their spiritual and personal development, and not being able to guide anyone to the truth for sound financial advice and guidance. More than half would end up miserable and broke.

Over the next several years, I would be employed with the City of Fort Wayne as a contract compliance officer, with the goal of ensuring that all majority contractors who won city bid awards, at least fifteen percent of all their federally funded contracts would go to minority subcontractors. After making spot visits at construction sites and attending our weekly Board of Works meetings (bid openings), it did not take long for me to get very frustrated with the system and what I saw was happening. Many times, a veteran contractor doing business with our city would simply start up a business in his wife's or other female's name and claim it as the subcontractor. Meeting with and seeing the disappointment and sometimes anger coming from many of our minority contractors was disheartening. I had no control, I could not help them, and I did not like it.

Politics? Never! I know that I had a huge bucket list, but getting involved in politics was not supposed to be one of them, or so I thought. In the early nineties, and early into his amazing public servant career, my youngest brother Joe was employed as an executive for our Wayne Township Trustee office. With his office located a block away from mine, I was familiar with their staff, was close to the elected trustee, and was acquainted with their purpose and efforts.

A township trustee is an official with authority who is elected over civil township government. The role of a trustee, or board of trustees, involves helping the poor with necessities if they have exhausted all other options of support. At this time, the trustee had unfortunately gotten involved in a tough situation and was going to be running for reelection; therefore, there was much concern in that township community about who would take over for him. I was asked if I would run. I emphatically answered NO!

After deep discussions with Joe, the township trustee, my family, and the Republican chairman, and after much prayer and with a profound concern for our citizens, I decided to run. To say that this was a huge undertaking was an understatement. Growing up in Fort Wayne, I have been blessed to have personal relationships with many of our local and state politicians, both Republicans and Democrats. This allowed me to cast my vote for their character, not their policies. With one-hundred percent funding from the Republican party, I decided to run under their umbrella. With a crowded field of primary candidates, I would go on to win the primary.

Soon after the primary victory, I got a firsthand look of the real side of politics. For the first time in my life, I saw the ignorance of people based on their political affiliations and stances. Even some of my close friends and relatives were looking at me differently. After several appearances and newspaper interviews, I would go on to be endorsed by both local newspapers, but I found myself not being excited about moving forward anymore.

I met with a few party leaders who strongly suggested who I should select as my office attorney and as a top staff executive when and if I won. I was not in agreement with them telling me who I could trust or select to work with. My opponent was someone who I liked and had a lot of respect for. I also knew he was more than capable of doing the job. The final straw came for me when both of our party leaders tried to dig up dirt on us and our families. It was strongly suggested that if we wanted to win, we needed to do this. What they did not know was that he and I had already spoken and had decided that as black men, we could not and would not let that happen.

Being transparent, I was in the middle of something I knew I would never and could never sell my soul to. The only thing I could do was to finish the race, and for the first time in my life hope and pray like hell that I lost. On election day, I could not wait to walk into my opponent's headquarters to personally congratulate him in front of his entire friends and party. To this day, I will tell anyone that the experience was one of the best and most valuable lessons of my entire life. It allowed me to find out who my true friends were and who really had my back.

In the early nineties, communities around the country were dealing with the senseless DWB (Driving While Black) virus, as thousands of black and brown citizens were being targeted and pulled over by police officers for no apparent reason. Communities were in an uproar. The only accountability of the police was the police policing themselves. It lacked integrity, was wrong, and was not working.

At this time, the mayor (a man I greatly respected) and our city's public safety director (a close friend of mine) asked me to consider working closely with Internal Affairs and become the city's first citizen to help monitor, take, record, flag, and report our community's police complaints. Many of those individuals and citizens were relatives and friends of mine, as were several of the police officers, black and white. My priority was to educate and make sure that all members of the community knew their rights and what they needed to do when stopped by the police. A few of the white officers were spreading rumors that I was out to get them, which could not have been further from the truth. I passionately believe and respect the law and have a huge appreciation for the sacrifice and work that they do. But have never had any respect for those who did and do not hold up to their "protect and serve" creed.

It was far more intense than I ever thought. After a long separation, I found myself finalizing my divorce, on top of running hard with my new Plan B deal I had just started. It was tough! As I ventured out to the community to host several Q&A community forums, the meetings would be well attended with plenty of concerns, complaints, and anger. And for some strange reason, a few uniformed police officers would show up, suggesting some form of intimidation—go figure! There were also not-so-subtle messages passed on to me though my friends and family; this was unacceptable and not cool. Mind you, the percentage of bad cops was low, but it was just enough to raise serious concerns for our entire community. Through an investigation, I found that many of these few had repeatedly been flagged for citizens' complaints (one had a total of eighteen), but little or nothing had been done about them, which boiled my soul. I totally understood why a few of the police felt the need to show up at my town meetings and try to intimidate me.

This was tough, but I felt strongly that it was it was an insult to my last name, courage, and integrity, as my obligation was to the citizens of our community, who depended on me to be trustworthy, strong, and transparent. Most of the community embraced, supported, and appreciated my efforts, though it was the most stressful job I ever had. It was a huge awakening to see firsthand just how our judicial system worked and did not work. In the absence of true accountability, and the presence of bullying and cover-up, there was unrest and madness. I simply did not want to be a part of that. During it all, I had determined that I needed to think outside the box, as I figured out that there had to be something more that the good Lord needed from me.

CHAPTER 16

No Big Fish

GROWING UP IN MY HOMETOWN WAS both a huge blessing and a huge challenge, as being six foot eight inches tall my entire adult life, there were not many places where I could go without being recognized. I found much love, respect, and appreciation for my accomplishments and for my service to our youth and community, but I also found a van load of jealousy and haters. As Jordans, we were always taught to expect, embrace, and use these as motivation. There will be no excuses for failure.

I soon found myself mentally and physically exhausted, feeling some form of depression; and unchallenged for the first time in my life. I was one who loved dreaming and waking up excited about my day. I was exhausted from trying to live up to others' expectations of me, with everyone thinking they knew me, folks lying about me (both good and bad), and many not respecting my privacy. I was exhausted! The worse part was that very few people understood my challenges, as they all assumed that I was void of personal demons and challenges, and that I was exempt from self-inflicted wounds.

Early in that year, I started attending business and mindset seminars. I was also reading many books such as Rich Dad, Poor Dad (Robert Kiyosaki); Awaken the Giant Within (Tony Robbins); See You at the Top (Zig Ziglar); Courage to Live Your Dreams (Les Brown); The 21 Irrefutable Laws of Leadership (John Maxwell); and others on mindset, entrepreneurship, multiple streams of income, plan Bs, and investing. I was excited about the possibilities and challenges of a new venture and firing my bosses.

I would also be elated and blessed by the news that I was going to be the father of my third child, a brilliant and gorgeous daughter number two (Arii). Like most of my life, the good Lord kept finding ways to drive and motivate me, even when I did not think that I needed any additional motivation. Though unexpected, my daughter has truly enriched and blessed me. I could not imagine her not being in my life.

Over the previous ten years, I had a serious debt with the IRS. While I was playing professional basketball, my agent had provided me with false documents and said that he had filed my taxes a few years prior, which he never did. I found this out though a shocking certified letter from the IRS. I was notified that I must contact them right away, and I had thirty days to pay them thirty thousand dollars. If not, they would be coming for my house and car and would be locking down my bank accounts, which was scary. I once again knew who I could call and lean on for strong locker room advice and guidance: my brother Charles. Though I was still overseas, I needed to try to save my house. Thank God that a payment agreement was reached. I spoke with many of my agent's other players, and we discovered that he had done the same exact thing to all of them. To make matters worse, he had filed bankruptcy and was no longer representing athletes. This was tough, as I had to form another game plan, pick myself up, think differently, bounce back, and challenge myself to put all the success principles to work. I knew that it was not going to be easy. I kept reminding myself that all roads to the top go straight though the dumps! The thousands of daily and nightly conversations with myself were painful, tearful, revealing, challenging, and yet motivational.

I finally figured out that I had to first fix me. Over my adult life, I always knew that I did not like being alone and single, with the games that came with dating many women. Looking back, it's funny how other people saw me. The thought of being in love and having that special someone that I could go home to at night at times had gotten me in trouble and led me to a few tough and questionable decisions. I had always been intrigued by the opposite sex, their strength, their touch, their grace, their motherly instincts, their wisdom, and their warmth. Plus, the cold fact was that they seemed to mature faster than many of us knuckle-headed men.

As I matured, I finally realized that I had been tremendously blessed with the quality of women that I had real friendships and relationships with and married. If nothing else, I knew that they were genuine friendships and love— even to this day. But the cold hard fact was that 99 percent of the bad stuff in my relationships had been my fault. For the most part, I had been blessed to have had good, strong women of high character in my life who cared for me. I would later find out that I simply was not man enough or ready to be the man that I needed to be during those times. I had to become better and stronger physically, mentally, and spiritually. It bought me pain to realize that some of my immaturity and self-inflicted wounds could have been avoided. After much prayer, I decided to turn most of my attention to developing my personal self-discipline by going after my new Plan B, which was coaching; developing my youth programs; and reading good books, especially the Bible. I also committed myself to taking an official pause from any kind of serious relationship or dating anyone for at least two years. That was my plan.

Ten months later, to help launch, promote, train, provide customer service, and build a strong team, I had invested in and opened a team training office in a mall in the south of town. Our team experienced rapid growth within a few short months. It was so rewarding to see our team become a family, to grow, to think outside of the box, to gain wealth principle knowledge, and to gain strength and confidence in knowing the importance of having a Plan B. I would receive word that I had to travel to Charlotte, North Carolina, for my first-ever national convention. Our team was going to be recognized for having one of the top customer acquisition organizations that quarter in the company. Also, I was being promoted to one of the top corporately earned positions within the company.

While I was planning the trip, I was disappointed to find out that I would have to go alone. My most beloved and respected traveling partner Edward Tharp (owner of a Shell gas station and a dry cleaner) and a few of our other top leaders could not get off work to attend with me. After all, I felt that it was a team award. As the leader of the pack, I knew that this was one more reason why I needed to be there. Getting a chance to hear from and be trained by one of my mentors, Mr. John Maxwell; seeing the first-class training; and being part of an enthusiastic crowd of 10,000 excited professional leaders blew me away. After three days of dark-thirty to dark-thirty training sessions, I was exhausted, but I could not wait to share with my team all that I had learned and seen, the people I had met, the incredible opportunity that was in front of us, and the mindset shift that had occurred for me that weekend. I can remember going into deep prayer that entire weekend, asking God to take my hand and lead me in whichever direction he chose. All weekend I kept hearing him say that he did not need me on somebody else's clock. I just knew that I had to get better, do better, and be better. I had no idea that the weekend would change my life in so many ways.

Waiting to board the flight back home, I met a doctor from Detroit who had been phenomenally successful with the company. He shared his story, his why, and his vision. I was so drained that I could not wait to get on the plane, draw my seat back, and doze off. But unbeknownst to me, the good Doctor Harris had changed his seat assignment to sit next to me. While everybody was boarding, he noticed an attractive young lady, Rhonda, looking for her seat. He could not and would not stop talking about her. He introduced both of us and started a deep and intriguing three-way conversation. I came to find out that she had just got started with our company and was attending her first-ever national convention as well. Rhonda was a CPA, a graduate of Marquette University, and an executive with Miller Brewing Company in Milwaukee, Wisconsin. She was pondering what kind of effort and game plan would help generate the kind of income she would need to leave her close to six-figure salary. During the flight, it reinforced many of the principles of successful people, as here was a doctor from Detroit and this phenomenally successful young lady still looking for a better quality of life. They were willing to do whatever they needed to do to get their time back. We all exchanged phone numbers and promised to be each other's accountability partner and assist each other whenever possible. By the way, I still did not get any sleep. God's plan!

CHAPTER 17

Next Play

OVER THIRTY YEARS AS A COACH, my kids have heard me yell (sometimes forcefully), "Next play!" a million times. It simply meant that they had no time to drop their heads, pout, or complain. They also could not question God, the officials, or their coach. Be a leader, be tough, be a good teammate, and quickly move to the next play. Now it was my turn.

Over the next year and a half, the young lady I met on the plane, Rhonda, and I would have thousands of deep business and personal phone conversations. We would talk about our faith, life challenges, mindsets, leadership, flaws, issues, past, failures, growth, lives, families, and personal development. We also discussed books we had read, company training nuggets, our goals, accountability, community, youth, my kids, and team building. We were also on top of being guest presenters on our separate team calls. We would travel back and forth to each other's hometown (Milwaukee and Fort Wayne) to headline in-house Super Saturday Training events. Our transparency had allowed us to quickly build trust, gain great respect for each other, become great friends, and make each other more productive and better. It is funny, but it was so refreshing that she did not like basketball and could not have cared less about my past sports accolades.

I was determined to stay committed to my two-year ban of not getting seriously involved in any relationship, but my close business partners across the country would try to convince me to ask Rhonda out on an official date. I had to admit that I had come to enjoy our relationship, her kindness, her spirit, the way she loved her family, her faith, her brilliance, and her intellect. One cold and snowy winter November weekend, as I traveled to Milwaukee to host a training event, it dawned on me that she made me better. Driving home, I decided that I needed to explore if I was ready to take a chance and ask her out, even with all my past relationship flaws and experiences. So, after several months of Rhonda playing hard to get and ignoring all my subtle hints, we became a couple.

Over the next couple of years, our businesses and relationship grew. We discovered that we both were desperately ready, and we wanted and needed to make a move from our hometowns. We both decided to trust God, step out of faith, leave our good jobs, partner our businesses together, and make our move. At the top of our list, we wanted to move to a diverse major market that was exploding economically where we could grow our business. And, of course, we wanted warm weather. It came down to either Dallas, Texas; or Atlanta, Georgia. Rhonda was assigned the task of flying into Atlanta to spend several days finding our first home; it was daunting. But the good Lord's plan and favor landed us in the home, community, and neighborhood he had just for us.

It was the fall of 2001. We were enjoying a few days out on the deck and kept hearing what sounded like a high school band practicing, as football season was right around the corner. We would discover two high schools literally a couple of blocks away.

Rhonda's cousin Debra would come by to welcome us and bring her son Armon to meet me, as he was fourteen, was six-foot-six and 220 pounds, and had a serious appetite for basketball. He immediately started to Google me. He would invite me to see him play his 8:00 A.M. AAU basketball game that Saturday morning. In Georgia, that meant that I would have to get up at the crack of dawn to get there on time. As my alarm went off, I was thinking of ways to get out of it, but Rhonda would not let me. She reminded me that Armon's dad was not in his life and that I had given my word to him. After finding the school, I noticed Armon's team was warming up on the far end of the gym, so I moved to position myself across from their team's bench. Before I could get to my seat, he had run from his team's layup line to greet me with a huge hug and an even bigger smile. I was so glad that I came!

Sitting there watching Armon's team beat down a team with CSA across their jerseys, a very personable young Caucasian lady, Charlene, whose son was playing for CSA, sat down next to me. Having witnessed that embrace between Armon and me, she asked if that was my son. I gave her a brief overview of our quick history and how I ended up there. She talked about her team's coach, her son and the other players on the other team, and her husband. If I were not watching the game, I would have thought they were the LA Lakers! My antenna went up a little when she began asking questions about my faith, my new home, and my family. She educated me on what that CSA (Christian Sports Association) stood for. I had to admit that talking to her helped me to get through the pain of watching those kids playing and getting a beat down like that. I was impressed by their attitudes, work ethic, and passion. Near the end of the game, she asked for my phone number. I was stunned, as it was something I never did. I do not know why, but I gave it to her.

The following Monday, I received a series of calls from an energetic, compassionate, and greatly confident coach of that CSA team, Mr. Gary Shaw. He asked me if I had a few minutes to meet with him and his partner behind the scenes of CSA. Within minutes, Rhonda and I were floored as Gary showed up at my front door and drove me to the meeting. I soon arrived at the beautiful neighborhood of million-dollar homes, literally ten minutes from my front door. Little did I know that they had researched me. They wanted to know if I would consider joining in their efforts to develop their youth sports program. I was mindful that the primary reason for our move to Georgia was to focus on growing our business, impacting others, and helping families live a better quality of life. It would be an understatement to say that I was impressed by their humbleness, vision, unbelievable wives (Kathy and Mary), love for family and community, and the God-fearing men that they were.

Gary's partner, George, had a huge vision and passion for Christian education and developing young people though Christ, while Gary's love for kids and sports would be hard to match by anyone's standards. Their children and wives were all connected by their spirit, faith, and love for community and each other. I loved their mission and quickly took over coaching, training, and mentoring the CSA team. Little did I know that I would fall in love with the kids' attitudes, work ethic, coachability, and desire to get better. They had quickly become our kids.

After a several weeks, our kids and team showed a tremendous amount of improvement and were able to muster up a several wins and at least compete with most of their opponents. Behind the scenes and without my knowledge, Gary, the Don King of promoting all of his kids from his adopted small North Cobb Christian (Class 1A) school, had been singing my praises and speaking with the leaders about having me join the school's high school varsity basketball staff as an assistant coach. We had no idea this school existed, but it was literally a one-minute drive from our new home. Gary and I would talk about kids, our faith, our families, and hoops for hours. We would quickly become brothers, as he would pick me up to go to different events and to view future land for purchase to build the CSA Sports Community Center. I loved those drives, as he would be so passionate about his vision and purpose that he would sometime forget where we were going and get us lost. Then he would laugh and say that he was just taking "the long cut." One day, he phoned and said that he was in a hurry, but he wanted to drop some paperwork off to me. He left his car running in the driveway, and 25 minutes later, he remembered that he left his car running and was now out of gas.

After prayer and deep discussion with Rhonda, I would meet with the knowledgeable, passionate, and impressive Head Coach Dorsey. The challenge was the time commitment that I had made with Rhonda to our business and to our business partners. They would accommodate my wishes by requiring me to attend only the practices and games, with no daily in-house teaching. I had been involved with kids in some form or fashion all of my adult life, so I was beginning to believe that the good Lord was not ready to let me out of that deal. The big kid that started all of this, Armon, would soon join our CSA team, transfer to North Cobb Christian, and later earn a full-ride scholarship to Liberty University to play basketball. Upon graduation, he would become a law enforcement officer in Atlanta. I am so proud of him!

It was now the summer of 2003, and Gary Shaw and the Donovan family had become important in our lives. Gary had called to inform me that he would be the hospital the next day for a heart valve replacement, but it was nothing to worry about. I had made plans to go see him that next evening. Then I received a call from our friend George, who informed me that Gary was not doing well, and that I probably should head to the hospital right away. As soon as I arrived in the hospital lobby, I was shocked to get the news that the good Lord had called Gary home. His spirit, his zest for life, and his love for his kids and his family I will never forget. I am forever grateful for his inspiration to be and do better. He has been missed tremendously by all who were blessed to know him.

Gary's passing motivated me even more to do everything I could to help make NCCS's basketball program a success. Upon arrival for the start of our pre-season workouts, I was informed that we would have a seasoned, senior-heavy roster. They were excited, great kids with super attitudes. I noticed that there were only two black kids in the entire basketball program. One black player on varsity, Darius Dunn, was a tremendous on-the-ball defender, excellent athlete, and outstanding leader; the other, Dustin Ware, was a middle-school eighth grader who probably was already the best basketball player and leader in the entire school. After getting to know their amazing parents, it was good to see that they were at NCCS because they believed in Christian education, wanted to ensure that their children got a great education, and loved the school. All the players seemed to get along, and they were excited about my being there, which ensured me that this was where the good Lord wanted me to be.

A few days later, the hype and the talk of the town was about three of the four of the top ten high school players in the entire country (future NBA players Dwight Howard, Patrick Ewing Jr., Josh Smith, and Morris Almond) were all attending school within twenty or thirty minutes of our home. I was even more excited to find out that top-ranked McEachern High School featuring Josh and Morris, and second-ranked Marietta High School featuring Patrick Ewing Jr., were slated to do battle that Friday. The media and everyone were saying that the game had been sold out for weeks, but as always, my faith kept telling me that I was supposed to be there anyway.

Driving up, I saw a line that was literally wrapped around the building, with no parking spot in sight. As I started to exit and head back, the car in the very last spot was pulling out. I took it as a sign. Walking to the back of the line, I heard a voice: "Walter Jordan?"

"Yes. You are?"

"I'm Larry. I met you years ago in Indianapolis at a Dustbowl tournament when I lived there."

"Wow! What are you doing here?"

"I've got an extra ticket. Do you need one?"

This was another sign that I was exactly where God wanted me to be. I saw three players who were freakishly gifted athletically, who played above the rim, and no doubt were headed to the NBA sooner rather than later. Being a product of great coaching, and from the basketball-crazy (below the rim) state of Indiana, in silence I reflected on what I did not see. I was wondering why kids with all this talent could not make free throws, had no mid-range games, could not handle the ball, and/or had no post moves. Now being officially involved in the Georgia basketball scene, I felt strongly that those guys were one in a million. Coach Dorsey and I felt that if I were to be involved with our kids and if we were going to compete in this state, we needed to find and develop kids who wanted to be basketball players, not just those who wanted to be on a team. We would have to find kids who were willing to be coachable and to grow, commit, learn how to play, compete, and become leaders. Though we had our work cut out for us, we were excited about the possibilities.

The first varsity season was rewarding and fun, as our senior-laden team worked hard and competed; but they did not have the talent or chemistry needed to overcome many of our weaknesses. But it was exciting to see our middle-school team, led by the eighth-grader Dustin Ware, finish their season unbeaten. It was amazing to watch, as 90 percent of the teams they faced were clearly more talented, bigger, and stronger, but Dustin had the unbelievable leadership ability and skill set to give all of his teammates confidence and to believe and play for each other.

After watching Dustin a few times, I knew that he was going to be special and somebody that we could build a program around. With my short experience the previous summer with the Georgia summer travel basketball landscape, I knew that it was going to be a serious challenge to keep him at NCCS (1A Christian school). The elite shoe-sponsored travel teams, fake promises, lies, and basketball wolves were coming.

Dustin's parents, Lisa and Nolan, had high character and were not going to be bought. They wanted only the best for their kids. Nolan and I had become great friends and had mutual respect. Our deepest conversation was about his being approached by one of Georgia's top 6A programs. He was not sure a school our size and with extremely limited athletic success or history could help Dustin reach his dreams, which was a real and huge question mark indeed. I leaned back on our faith, trust, commitment, and vision, with this question: "Are you telling me that God can't get him where he wants to go from here at NCCS?" With Nolan's commitment, we knew that it was time to form a concrete plan, year-round training, and a positive environment. We would build a competitive travel squad that our parents could trust, so our kids could grow and get better.

I would also create my Hoop School (skills, leadership, and mindset training) and a summer travel team, focusing on the development of the three NCCS returning seniors. It was urgent and important that they understood what would be expected of them, what things were non-negotiable as leaders, and what work was going to be required if they wanted to reach their goals. They would team up with kids from several other high schools, work their butts off, improve tremendously, make new friends, and have a great summer. My additional purpose was to follow all of them during their senior season and to do everything I could to help them to prepare for and find college hoop homes.

The first day of our preseason training practice, our young ninth graders, four returning varsity players, and three new enrollees who were all solid contributors immediately seemed to have a special bond. The daily encouragements, discipline, accountability, positive conversations, energy, character, and selfishness displayed during scrimmages quickly allowed these strangers to become friends and solid teammates. Our entire coaching staff was blown away by the respect that all our kids had for each other, and how quickly our obvious and a few unexpected leaders showed up. They were fully aware that our regional and cross-town archrival Fellowship Christian's senior-laden team was loaded and would be ranked number one in the state. And soon-to-be state rivals, Deerfield Academy of Albany, Georgia, would also be loaded and favored to meet Fellowship in Macon, Georgia, for the state championship.

The season would be one of great growth, discovery, and development, as the guys would embrace the process, gain unbelievable confidence, and sacrifice for each other. Fellowship Christian would dominate our region and would be seeded number one after beating us on their home floor early in the conference season. They would later return with a hard-fought victory, followed by a never-to-forget massive victory celebration in front of our home fans. Our players, fans, and coaching staff were not happy campers!

As we prepared for the state tournament, our kids had found their identity and learned to trust each other. They found their sway and were hungry and determined to play for each other. We would move on to advance to the Final Four to battle the pre-season state champions favorite Deerfield Academy, led by mister do-everything, freshmen sensation Andre Young.

By then, a boatload of my college coaches' friends and contacts had gotten word that I was coaching and residing in Georgia. They began to contact me, asking about players who had caught their attention and getting my opinion of them. If I did not know, I would attempt to find out, as I loved trying to help talented and quality kids with high character to connect with coaches and programs.

A day before heading to Macon for the Final Four, I received a call from an assistant coach from Georgia asking about Andre Young. Without hesitation, I informed him that the two best point guards in the entire state of Georgia would be going head-to-head on Friday night. He responded by asking who the other one was. I left him with this: "Coach, you may be coming to the game to check out Andre, but you'll leave talking about Dustin Ware!"

The game and the matchup did not disappoint, as Dustin once again found a way to be the coach on and off the floor, making his teammates better, getting everybody involved, and making all the big plays. We would move on to play a very well-coached team and our cross-town rivals, Fellowship Christian, for the 2003 GHSA 1A State Championship.

By the way, en route to home, I received another call from that Georgia coach who couldn't stop asking me about Dustin. He also mentioned that he had just gotten off the phone with Coach Dennis Felton, who was going to be changing his schedule to attend the next night's championship game. I was blown away, and I knew that I could not let this get out to this young fifteen-year-old kid as he was preparing to play in the biggest game of his life.

The championship battle's first half was tense, ugly, and tight, as the senior-laden Fellowship team was under tremendous pressure as the heavy favorites after going undefeated in our region. We had sold our kids on the fact that all the pressure would be on them. With our youth, we felt that if we could keep it close in the first half, catch our breath, and relax, our shots would start to fall and we would have a chance in the second half. NCCS's amazing student body, parents, faculty, and fans once again chartered buses to be there to support their team. The players were determined to give it everything they had. Every loose ball, rebound, and shot was hotly contested on both sides, as the teams battled back and forth. In the middle of the game, I found myself thinking about my good friend Gary Shaw and how proud he would have been of these kids.

It is not often that the big game exceeds the hype of the game, but I don't remember the cheer block from either team sitting down the entire game. The whole time, Dustin would settle for keeping everyone involved on the offense end of the floor. As we entered the third overtime, we felt that no one was in better physical condition than we were.

We also knew that if we were going to became state champs, our key players would have to make some big plays down the stretch. I reminded Dustin of two things during the game that his dad, Nolan, would always tell him. Number one: "It's not about your age, but about your game!" And number two: "It was time for him to take over!" And that he did. The fans and coaches of both teams were totally drained, well soaked (as if we had played), and emotionally spent. In three consecutive trips down the floor, Dustin would call for a high pick-n-roll (his favorite and our money play), and he would nail back-to-back-to-back three pointers to secure the trophy. To say NCCS's Dustin Ware was no longer an afterthought or a secret would be an understatement!

The coaching staff knew that we would be losing our talented senior big man, Jody Jenkins (Berry College), and our solid stretch four man, Jon Kessler (SPSU—Georgia Tech), and one of our top three guards. These were huge losses for a team that had little quality depth and size to begin with. But NCCS's culture, foundation, environment, and brand were set.

The 2005 season began with a surprise announcement that our head coach had stepped down. They needed me to step up to be the head coach, even though they know that I could not commit to being a full-time staff member and teacher. We embraced the challenge. The staples of our brand continued: striving to be never be out-worked, emphasizing team defense, having each other's back, and playing for each other.

Most of our kids had no desire to move on to play collegiate basketball, but we could never tell as we watched them fight for each other every second they took the floor. The obvious love, pride, and respect they had for each other and their school was a joy to witness. There was no question that their character and attitude would serve them well in the future.

Despite our many challenges, this team would make it all the way to the Final Four, upsetting a couple of strong Macon, Georgia, teams en route to losing to a nail-biter in the semi-final game. It was one of my most rewarding and fun times coaching in my career.

By the way, Dustin Ware would be offered a full-ride scholarship to attend his dream school, the University of Georgia, during his sophomore season. Because of his strong DNA, he would give his word and stay committed. He would play for and become a UGA college graduate.

During that season, I also had a chance to view many quality games, as I was looking to hand pick a strong group of talented and high-character sophomores and their parents in the area who wanted to commit to join our travel team. I knew once I got them together in the gym, they would see our game plan and find out that we already had the best leader and point guard in the state on the roster. They were going to work their butts off, get better, grow, play together, respect each other, have fun, and do every-thing they could to reach their dreams of playing at the next level. Thus, our non-profit Team Impact—Georgia travel organization was founded. One hundred percent of the parents and players I met with showed interest, trusted us, and committed to locking arms for the next three years to see what we all could accomplish for our kids together. I was humbled! Competing at a highest level around the globe against the best of the best; earning serious respect from their peers, opposing coaches, and college coaches everywhere; and seeing them reach their goals of going to college and earning their degrees, set the bar high for our Team Impact organization for years to come.

Our 2006 school year started with a couple of huge surprises, as right before the first day of school, we received word that one of our Team Impact players, Matt Shaw, a six-foot-six stud, had enrolled in NCCS, as he loved playing with Dustin and felt that I could help him reach his dreams of playing college basketball. Shortly afterward, two other kids, who were strangers to me, had also enrolled to attend. The team included tremendously tough and strong role models. Team-first guys were returning, led by lock-down defensive specialist Darius Dunn, Stephen Keesler (with a school record of 24 offensive charges in a season), tenacious David Cooley, and several other outstanding athletes.

By now, the word had gotten out about North Cobb Christian basketball and Dustin Ware. With the light, magnitude, and growth of our program, I knew that I could not continue to be a part-time head coach. That was when I was approached by Greg Matta, an assistant coach at Kennesaw State University, who was looking to get into high school coaching. I knew of Greg from his family name and from attending KSU games. I knew that he was also the younger brother of then Ohio State's Head Coach Thad Matta. After several conversations, it did not take long to feel his passion for kids and his love of basketball. With both of us being from the Midwest (Illinois and Indiana), we talked about the history of the game, our former coaches, our visions, our philosophies, and the challenges of becoming champions.

Coach Matta had the fire, enthusiasm, passion, knowledge, and documentation. He could also fulfill the need of being an in-house educator and a full-time staff member. He agreed to take over as head coach, and I agreed to be his assistant. I know that decision would make my wife happy. But I also felt it was the best thing for our kids, my health, our business, and the future of our program. Once again, it confirmed my philosophy that teamwork always works!

Knowing that we had two to three Division One prospects on our roster, we upgraded our schedule to include several big-time programs and high-profile players. Our guys proved to be up to the challenge, as they finished unbeaten and won our second state championships in three years!

The next season, we were blessed to with two players from Serbia, Milos Kleut and Stephon Franks, who moved in and enrolled. Our roster (Akil Morrow, Romeo Lewis, Stephen Kessler, David Cooley, and Matt Mendell) was loaded with talent. Led by our awesome senior leadership, and now playing against 5A teams, we would finish 35–0, winning our third state championship in four years and topping it off by winning the National Championship.

Over those fifteen years I served as head coach, as assistant coach, and in other basketball positions. Rhonda and I would become like family to not only the basketball teams, but also to our total student body. Many of the players would touch my heart in every way and become long-time friends through weddings, graduations, college degrees, life successes, and hardships. The most rewarding and fulfilling accomplishments were seeing more than 90 percent of them go on to attend college, with many earning a chance to play basketball collegially. Many of the parents, such as the Donovans, Gary and Kathy Shaw, Lisa and Nolan Ware, Annette and Stanford Dunn, Sheronda and Tony Butt, Sallie and Steve Shaw, William Credit, Stephanie Hargett, Megan and Clint Strange, Jenny and Mark Henry, Ros and Roland James, Jim Turner, the Mattas, the Symithias, the Geters, and the Bambas, would become treasured and loved friends for life. Whatever God has for you, he has just for you!

That initial Team Impact team would field every one of our kids, helping them earn a chance to fulfill their dreams of attending and playing college basketball. That roster and their colleges selected: JC Ward (Marietta High School / Tennessee State University); Dustin Ware (NCCS / Georgia); Matt Sundberg (Harrison High School / College of Charleston); Stanley Jennings (Marietta High School / Albany State); Matt Shaw (NCCS / Lipscomb); Blake Cain (Harrison High School / Costal Carolina); Ryan Bayersdorfer (Harrison High School / Georgia); Matt Mendall (NCCS / Georgia Southwestern); Nick Hardy (Coosa / Chattahoochee Tech); and Lovell Cook (South Cobb / New Orleans).

The parents, our kids, and their successes spearheaded a serious word-of-mouth campaign to encourage me to start a program to assist other parents who may want to have their kids develop as student athletes and leaders. Learning to hear God, the following year over two hundred kids of all ages showed up for tryouts. Completely blown away, a brand-new game plan was quickly revamped. I felt strongly that if God bought them to me, I needed to figure it out.

Now, sixteen years later, we have been blessed to see our seasonal travel hoops program expand to between 150 and 170 kids (15 to 17 teams) in any given summer. Well over 150 of our kids have gone on to play college sports, both football and basketball. Over 200 have attended college, with 150 of them earning degrees. There have been two NFL first-round draft picks (Hunter Henry for the Chargers and Bradley Chubb for the Broncos) and several European professional basketball players (Dustin Ware, Lovell Cook, Stephon Jelks, and others). We now boast an aerospace engineer, a pilot, educators, attorneys, corporate executives, real estate investors, business owners, real estate agents, coaches, community leaders, husbands, and excellent fathers. Look at God!

CHAPTER 18

Devastation

HEARTBROKEN! ON SEPTEMBER 16, 2004, A day I will never forget, I received word that the good Lord had called my best friend, my 28-year-old son Jamarcus, home. Three years prior to this, he had been diagnosed with lymphoma. Through it all, I had witnessed his unbelievable, never wavering, and rock-solid faith. Even through his pain and insane storm, his positive attitude, uplifting spirit, selfless heart, and unfailing strength were true testaments of who he had been his entire short life.

After attending Anderson College in Indiana for several years, he and the now famous Heather Hadley, his extremely talented friend and high school classmate, who was attending Northwestern University, decided to leave school and head to the bright lights of New York to pursue their passion and dreams of Broadway and the big lights. They had performed together during their high school days. All his life I had preached to him to follow his passion, to be himself, to keep God first, to treat people right, and to dream big. He totally understood the odds, sacrifices, and challenges that were in front of him, but he was excited about them. Forever the optimist, his faith, determination, and attitude never allowed him to have any doubt or to look backward; he was all in! Despite my struggling with the idea of him living in New York, and all the many challenges that came with it, I had to suck it up and encourage, support, and pray for them. Knowing my son, I would not bet against him.

Jamarcus was a young man who absolutely loved his siblings, mom, grandparents (Rose and Lorenzo), and family. The older he got, the more it would blow me away when he shared his personal, private, and often sensitive life challenges and decisions about his life. As we both traveled the world following our dreams, there were only a few birthdays when he was not the first person to call me (sometimes at six A.M.) to wish me a happy birthday and tell me that he loved me. It was important to him, and meant the world to me.

In his last couple of years with him fighting for his life, his mom, grandma, and I tried to encourage him to come back home to Indiana so his family could help with his medical and daily needs. But he felt that New York was now his home. In hindsight, I now realize he felt as if he would have been burden of us. Of course, nothing could have been further from the truth.

My toughest moments occurred the numerous times when I traveled to Columbia Presbyterian Hospital to visit with him, as he went back and forth during his struggles. It was hard to see him connected to all those machines. He was in massive pain while trying to be strong, to smile, and to show some love to everybody who came to see him, especially his mom and grandma. In private, I would tell him that it was okay to cry, and not try to be Superman. When he was there, I would always plan to stay with him the entire time I was in New York. At night while I attempted to sleep in a chair and watched him sleep, I would cry worse than an infant.

Days before his homegoing, he called sounding better than he had in a long time. He started the conversation by sharing with me how much he loved his family and our relationship, and that he was tired and was ready to go home. He proceeded to ask me to get a pen and paper, as he wanted to let me know that he wanted me to speak at his funeral service. He even told me what he wanted me to wear, down to his favorite tie. Not long after that, on September 16, 2004, he received his wings. Devastated!

Without fail, every time we talked, he would start by asking how I was doing with my health and telling me to make sure I was taking care of myself. I was so in awe of who he was, his strength, and all the things he stood for. He taught me so much, even in those unimaginable times. To this day, I sometimes feel tears running down my checks as I am filled with mixed emotions of pain, laughter, and gratitude. By the way, his dear friend, Ms. Heather Hadley, was in the middle of a national tour but found a way to attend and perform at his service. I am quite sure that Markie was smiling, singing, and dancing that day. No more pain! Thank you, Lord!

A few years prior to this, I received a phone call from a friend letting me know that he had just started his own life insurance company. He asked if I would consider letting him handle my life insurance, and of course, I did. We would schedule a house exam and go from there. Several days later, I received a call that I had failed the test and needed to get to a doctor as soon as possible. With my family history of losing my mom and dad to cancer, I was very fearful, as I dreaded that "C" word. After a few days, we received the results of the blood work and tests. I was informed that I was a full-blown diabetic and had to make serious lifestyle changes right away. I was not over-weight, I was exercising three to four days a week, and I was feeling fine, so my doctor and I were surprised by the results. Looking back on my life-long terrible eating habits and soul food cravings, I should not have been surprised. Though shocked in this case, my good friend truly served as a life-saving benefit.

It was early August 2006, and my first three-year team of rising elite seniors was excited and getting ready to fly out to Las Vegas for their very last college live recruiting opportunity. The big-time college coaches and recruiting services were going to be there.

My wife Rhonda had scheduled my quarterly diabetic doctor's visit a couple of days prior to our flight. The doctor insisted that I undergo an EKG before I left. One day after that appointment while I was preparing for the next day's flight, I kept seeing my doctor's name and number on my phone, which was unusual, as my doctor had never called me before. I figured that I would give him a call when I returned from Vegas. A few hours later, his nurse called Rhonda and told her to get me to the Emergency Room right away. Shaken and upset, she was disappointed that I had not answered my phone when the doctor called.

When we arrived at the hospital, we were informed that three of my arteries were 75 to 90 percent blocked or more. Still not understanding or not wanting to hear the severity, I ask the doctor if I could take care of it when our team returned from Vegas the following week. He got my attention when he stated, "If you get on that plane heading to Vegas, you probably won't make it back!" As Mom used to say, "Men plan; God laughs!"

Although I was feeling well for fifty years old, I was immediately admitted to the hospital. After a series of nerve-wracking tests and scans, it was determined that they would have to perform what was now emergency quadruple bypass heart surgery.

Rhonda would call my brother Charles, who lived seventy miles away in Winder, Georgia, to let the family know. Like always, it did not take long for him to arrive. Rhonda also immediately contacted our other coaches and parents to let them know what was happening. An hour or so later, my hospital phone began ringing off the hook, and the waiting room was overflowing with former and current players, NCCS students, parents, and friends. The nurses and doctors who were making their rounds would stop and ask, "Who are you? Are you a celebrity of some kind?" I would respond that I was no one special, but I just knew I lot of great people. Rhonda and Charles would take charge, canceling almost all visitors until after my recovery, taking my cell phone, and having the telephone removed from my room.

Around this time, a sharp, black, and distin-guished-looking head cardiothoracic surgeon, Dr. William Cooper, was making his nightly rounds and inquired about me and what was going on. We would have a brief conver-sation. Unbeknownst to me, he had instructed his staff to clear his schedule, as he was personally going to perform my surgery.

You can probably imagine that there were many reasons why I did not sleep well that night, but the fact that my bed was two feet too short did not help. Of course, as only he could do, Charles raised holy hell about it; a day later, my new extra-long bed arrived.

One of my toughest memories was seeing the look on Rhonda's face when the doctors went over the proce-dures and possible outcomes, including mentioning that at some point during the surgery, my heart will need to stop beating. I will never forget that look while she watched me sign the consent forms. That night, I went into deep conversations with my angel (mom) and with my Lord and Savior Jesus Christ. I asked the good Lord to grant me just a little more time, as I had some unfinished business that I needed to fix. I needed more time to try to be and do better as a father and a person, to touch a few more lives, and to make sure that Rhonda, my kids, my family, and friends knew just how much I loved them. That night it really hit me just how much I had taken time for granted.

The next morning as I headed to surgery, I found myself surprisingly at peace, as my faith told me that I would not be in that room alone. A few hours later, the good Lord had heard and granted me more time. Hallelujah! When I awoke, the buzz around the recovery room was how I had been smiling in my sleep immediately after the surgery. What they did not know was that I had just had the most amazing out-of-body experience in my life. I believed that I had just seen and spoken to my son, my mom, and my dad. We expressed how much we loved each other, and the fact that God was not ready for me yet. Until now, I have shared this with only a few close family members, as I knew that it would test most nonbelievers. The good Lord had bought me to my knees, humbled me, and gave me my marching orders. He had my attention. Thank you, Lord!

CHAPTER 19

Celebration of Life

FINALLY, AFTER THREE EXTRA-MISERABLE DAYS IN the hospital due to an unknown infection, I was released to go home. I could not wait to sleep in my own bed, and more importantly, to eat some food I could at least taste (though restricted) and enjoy. A week later, I was hit with an incredible and awesome surprise, as several of my best friends and Purdue classmates (Fred Arrington, Raymond Odom, Ronnie Moore, and Jerome King) had flown into town to spend a few days with me. I was not sure my heart could handle those three fun-filled days, but I will never forget them. It was as if we were all back in West Lafayette with plenty of trash-talking and good-natured card playing, lies, love, and laughter. I laughed so much and so hard that Rhonda would come and check on me several times. She would later mention just how blessed and loved I was!

I was inundated with phone calls. Unbeknownst to me, Rhonda and Charles (the two wings beneath my wings) had started putting plans together for a Celebration of Life weekend celebration in Atlanta. I was now fifty-one years old, but I never had a birthday party, so this was totally out of my comfort zone. After deep conversions with them both, I was told that it was not about me, but it was about sharing, educating, encouraging, and motivating black men and my close friends to live a better quality of life. I was told that all they needed me to do was show up. Rhonda and Charles would contact my closest friend who would rally the troops. I began to think that this was part of my purpose and what the good Lord would want me to do. I was learning to hear God.

WE ARE FAMILY
by Charles Jordan

As you all know, last year Walt found himself with a heart illness so serious that it required him to undergo major open-heart surgery. Many of you called, visited, and prayed for his recovery. God answered our prayers and has allowed us the pleasure of fellowshipping with our brother again.

This "Celebration of Life" event is the idea of his wife Rhonda. During Walt's illness, surgery, and recovery, she has been his strength and the wind beneath his wings. Walt has mentioned that he believes God spared his life so he can reach out and help other people become more aware of the dangers of an unhealthy lifestyle. He also mentioned that he wanted this to be a celebration, not about him, but about all his close friends.

The unhealthy lifestyle in which we engage extends far beyond the physical and the diet, but to the spiritual and mental as well. All of this affects our ability to perform at the genius level. During the weekend, we hope to accomplish the following objectives: 1) Get reacquainted; 2) Laugh, joke, and tell a few lies; 3) Eat, drink, and be merry; 4) Engage in some meaningful, uplifting discussions and possible solutions and game plan for all of us to strive to live a better quality of life for our loved ones and each other.

On August 10–12, 2007, in Atlanta (almost a year after my heart surgery), the "Walter Jordan's Celebration of Life" two-day celebration was held. This included a Friday night meet-and-greet and dinner at Barnacle's Sports Bar & Grill, Saturday morning breakfast, Saturday afternoon Celebration of Life cookout, health and wellness discussions, and more fellowship. On Friday afternoon, a busload of successful, God-fearing and Team Jordan brothers started flowing in from around the country: Isiah Murray (entrepreneur), Terrance Howard (real estate agent), Willie Credit (high school coach), Jamaal Greer (educator), George Forrest (McDonald's franchise owner), Buck Jenkins (educator), Al Marshall (corporate sales), Carlton Green (youth director), Eric Watkins (paralegal), Stanford Dunn (Comcast executive), Sharif Colbert (music producer), Max Richardson (attorney), and Jerome King (college official). The Jordan crew of Willie, Charles, Lafayette, Art, Joe, and nephew Jason were also on hand. The evening highlights included everyone sharing how we met and connected, and the depth of our relationships. The lies were almost as big as the laughter, and the laughter was intense! My heart was filled, and it had been only a few hours.

The next afternoon, our close friend, big-time realtor and sister Sharon Nibbs, hosted an amazing cookout in her spacious and beautiful home. On a breathtaking fall Georgia day, her deck was the perfect setting for a celebration of any kind. To top it off, my childhood best friend

Raymond Causey (now a pastor), Purdue teammates Eugene Parker (NFL agent/attorney) and Joe Berry Carroll (number 1 NBA draft choice/author), Nolan Ware (entrepreneur), Argentry Reese (finance), and several other guests blessed all of us with their presence. Charles set the agenda and expectations for the day. All the guests introduced themselves and shared how we were connected. Rhonda shared her amazing tear-jerking recap of my heart surgery episode week and her love for me.

The sharing of some personal and family health challenges and conversations was intense, emotional, and heartfelt, yet it set the tone for encouragement, motivation, and inspiration for us to all commit to do better. One of the subjects was "Are you ready to die?" To a man, we all agreed that we were not ready to die, but we agreed that at the end the deeper, bigger, and most important question was "Are you prepared to die?" After powerful personal testimonies, deep references to scriptures, and passionate discussions, we all agreed that we had some unfinished business before we were prepared for the good Lord to call us home. It was during those tough-love moments that I received confirmation of why God needed and allowed our celebration weekend to happen.

Fifteen years later, now at age sixty-five, I am extremely grateful to have had the opportunity for many of my closet friends to meet, bond with, know, and fellowship with each other. But the most important thing is for us to express our zest for life and our love for our Lord and Savior Jesus Christ and for each other. Each day that passes, the time spent with my friends means more and more to each of us, as four of my dynamic brothers (Eugene Parker, Isiah Murray, Ronnie Moore, and Terrance Howard) have gone on to be with the Lord. I am comforted by the fact that they all knew the Lord and were prepared when God called them home. My fight is still ongoing, and I too pray that I will be prepared and ready. Thank you, Lord!

CHAPTER 20

The Fool, the Victim, the Kingdom

BEFORE EACH OF US OFFICIALLY ENTERS this world, we enter as a member of somebody's team. When we leave this world, we will leave as a member of somebody's team. Good, bad, or indifferent, what happens in between those two dates will bring pain, love, tears, challenges, respect, heartaches, confusion, exhilaration, victories, defeats, sorrows, and prayerfully through it all, growth. Some people experience these things more than others. For me, each day contributes to what I have called a full and blessed life.

At times I describe my life in three phases, with my first, *The Fool,* being my foolish stage. That was the time in my life when I was young, prideful, selfish, and egotistical and when I did not realize my stuff stunk. It was a time when my boys and I had so much fun that there should have been a law against some of the stuff we did; in fact, a couple of those things probably did!

There were times when I took success, people, love, God, family, time, kids, relationships, and my health for granted. At age seventeen, many times in secret, I was mentally and emotionally using my mom's death as excuses to do foolish things and not honoring her the way I knew that I should have. There was nothing criminal, nothing intentional, and nothing spiteful, but I was just reckless in thought, understanding, or consideration of all parties involved. I was so blessed that I was surrounded by some amazing friends (male and female), teammates, and brothers who loved to have fun, laugh, and party; who cared for each other; and who knew there was always a line that we could not and would not cross. A wise man avoids all fools when in the pursuit of wisdom, happiness, and the Kingdom. "A fool takes no pleasure in understanding, but only in expressing his opinion" (Proverbs 18:2).

My second phase of life is the one I often refer to as **The Victim.** It was the phase when I found myself having pity parties and not understanding why tough challenges, heartaches, and devastations were happening to me. It took a fair amount of time for me to stop blaming God for the pain, fight, and suffering that my mom, dad, and son went through prior to their deaths. At one point, I was so lost that I found myself pointing fingers and blaming God for my injuries during my professional basketball dreams and goals.

In between times, I had been blessed to be involved with three special ladies (including two that I married), who loved, respected, and cared about me deeply. Obviously, being so lost, I was blinded by the fact that I was not being true to myself, did not know who I was, and was simply not mentally, emotionally, or physically prepared the way they deserved and needed me to be. The pain that I still endure from traveling around the globe chasing my dreams, and the precious times I missed with my children, still hurts my heart. Those are precious moments I will never get back. I was blaming others, God, and everyone else when it was blatantly obvious that all of all those issues were self-inflicted. I still pray about these things daily.

Victimizing oneself is a terrible disservice to your heart. It allows you to place false blame on others and to become a frightening and paralyzing force that blocks your blessing and follows you everywhere you go.

My third phase is called **The Kingdom.** This is the phase that I believe everyone should be striving to reach, no matter what it takes or how long it takes to get there. The key is not procrastinating and gambling with the time we may or may not have left to get there. Every knee must bow down, and every tongue must confess!

I pray that anyone reading this without God that he will bring you to your knees as he did me, that you will bow down and confess your sins, and that you will learn to love our Lord and Savior. In August of 2006, I was unexpectedly rushed into the emergency room needing quadruple bypass heart surgery. The night prior to surgery, all I could think and pray about was the people I was not yet sure knew how much I loved and appreciated them. I also thought about my kids that I needed to apologize to for not always being there. I also needed to ask God to forgive me for not serving, honoring, and praising him the way I should have. I asked for his forgiveness and promised him that if he granted me just a little more time, I would turn my life over to him and that I would be and do better.

As still a sinful, flawed, and fragile man, there is not a day that goes by that I do not praise God. I want to be his servant, show my love for everybody, strive to be a better human being, and fulfill his plan and purpose for my life. Thank you, Lord!

"If my people who are called by my name humble themselves, and pray and seek my face, and turn from their wicked ways, then I will hear from heaven and will forgive their sin and heal their land" (2 Chronicles 7:14).